ZonePerfect Cookbook

ZonePerfect
cookbook
by kristy walker

Text and Recipes: Kristy Walker
Editor: Elizabeth Penn
Copy Editor: Lynda Zuber Sassi
Design and Layout: Platinum Design, Inc. NYC
Photographs: StockFood, FoodPix and Peter Johansky

ISBN: 1-930603-92-4

Printed and bound in Singapore

acknowledgments

The idea for this book came about due to so many requests from the students in my classes for a ZonePerfect cookbook. People wanted to camp out at my house just to see how I cook my meals. I was embarrassed at the idea of people watching me cook, as I do not think of myself as a chef. However, I do know how to keep meals simple, healthy, and tasting good.

I also know that over time, people might want some interesting twists and surprises with their ZonePerfect meals, so I have the good fortune of working with two natural food chefs, Janet Hampel and Alana Sugar. This book would not have been written without their help. We all spent many late nights and weekends creating recipes and getting the portions into ZonePerfect balance. Janet and Alana have created some of the more elaborate, gourmet recipes for you to enjoy. These recipes will be especially fun when you entertain guests while using the ZonePerfect Nutrition Program.

One of the most important people who helped me manifest this book is Linda Anderson, my personal editor. It's incredible to find someone who can take your words, rewrite them, and have them come out as your heart felt them originally.

Chris Baker, chief executive officer of ZonePerfect Nutrition Company, I want to thank you for your support, encouragement, and introducing me to the right contacts to make this book happen.

I also want to thank all of the following folks for their huge amounts of support:

My daughter, Jenny; my mom and dad, Mary and Joe Walker; Robin Bruce, Kathy Bruce, Shelley Lane De Courtin, Kinsloe Queen, Don Ginn, Edna Bowen, Paul Pruett (He kept asking me, how's that book going?), Caran Wysong, Bob Hays, Sandra Bowen, Susan Bremer, Debra and Jay Templeton, Virginia Goszewska, Lo Whipple, Jerry Young, Leslie James, Kent Livingston, Dr. Dan Rosen, Dr. Paul Kahl, Misha, Isabella, and Harold and Joan Klemp.

I understand now that to manifest anything worthwhile truly takes a village, and then some.

table of contents

about
kristy walker

Kristy Walker, B.S., Certified ZonePerfect Instructor, is the national sales manager for the ZonePerfect Nutrition Company. She is a health educator, consultant, international workshop facilitator, researcher, and writer. Kristy has worked in the natural foods industry for over 20 years with the goal of maximizing the health potential of others. She is listed in the *Who's Who of American Women*.

Kristy has taught thousands of people how to make conscious food choices through the ZonePerfect Nutrition Program with an emphasis on natural and organic foods. Carefully assessing individual needs, she provides her clients with powerful tools and motivation for making life-long, healthy changes.

introduction

One day, I realized that I'd grown tired of hearing myself ask, "How am I going to lose weight and be healthy too?" Any time I had space between thoughts, my attention would drift to health and weight loss. I wondered if I'd be asking this question until I was 120 years old. How truly boring!

The next day, while taking my daily time for quiet reflection, I asked with deepest sincerity, "If there is a system that will help me, please show me what it is. I'll do it!"

Soon after I asked to be shown a way of eating that would work for me, I found the ZonePerfect Nutrition Program. According to its website, ZonePerfect is defined as a nutrition program that was developed to help people quickly and easily achieve and maintain their health and fitness goals. The program uses research in science and nutrition to harness the powerful, almost drug-like effects of food, in order to position your body within a hormonally controlled zone almost 24 hours a day.

After studying the elements of the ZonePerfect Nutrition Program, I learned that to achieve and maintain maximum good health and weight loss, a balanced proportion of proteins, carbohydrates, and fats is necessary. ZonePerfect was the system I had been looking for. Following this simple system would enable me to have weight loss combined with building up a healthy, infection-fighting immune system and feeling energized!

I began to prepare my meals and snacks in the balanced and proportional way of eating that ZonePerfect recommends. This meant that at every meal or snack, 30 percent of the calories came from protein, 40 percent from carbohydrates, and 30 percent from fats. Within six months, I had lost 30 pounds and tons of inches. As a bonus, I had more energy than ever.

my weight loss journey

For years, I'd been listening to an old song playing inside my head. Maybe you'll recognize the tune: When am I going to figure out how to lose weight? How can I become healthier? What program should be my lifetime way of eating? I seemed to be looking for the Holy Grail of healthy, permanent weight loss!

By the time I found ZonePerfect, I'd been working for over twenty years in the natural food industry and I'd learned a thing or two:

* **SUGAR IS A BAD THING,**
* **CERTAIN FATS IN THE DIET ARE NECESSARY,**
* **EXERCISE IS IMPORTANT,**
* **ORGANIC PRODUCE IS HEALTHIER FOR OUR BODIES AND OUR PLANET**
* **WATER IS A NECESSITY FOR THE BODY.**

Yet, even armed with all of this knowledge, something still held me back from achieving weight loss and a healthy lifestyle.

My journey to healthy weight loss and maximizing my energy took many twists and turns. I was a vegetarian for many years. Then I switched to macrobiotic cooking. I experimented with food allergy testing, acupuncture, fasting, homeopathy, body chemistry balancing, and vitamin/mineral therapy. I tried Chinese, Korean, Ayurvedic, American, and South American herbs, and imagination work. I joined diet programs. I tried prescription diet pills and even had hormonal testing. Still, I failed to achieve my personal health goals and became increasingly confused and frustrated.

From each system, like a bee fluttering from flower to flower, I gathered the sweet nectar of weight-loss wisdom. Though I applied what worked from each program, I still couldn't get where I wanted to be or maintain the weight loss.

Before getting involved in the natural foods industry, I had studied and received a degree in criminal justice. This background caused me to be curious about the influence that diet might have on human behavior. *Maybe*, I thought, *if I could understand the effects that food has on mood, behavior, and energy levels, I'd discover the secret to eating well.* My studies suggested that food's relationship to the body's hormonal system held the key to this secret.

After my first week of following the ZonePerfect Nutrition Program, with its attention to keeping the hormonal system balanced, I experienced the plan's effects on weight loss. To my surprise, those ginger snap cookies on top of the refrigerator no longer tempted me! Before this, I believed those cookies to be healthy, since they contained no hydrogenated oils or processed sugar. I did not realize that these cookies were high-glycemic carbohydrates and would promote hunger and unbalance my hormones.

After I began the ZonePerfect way of eating, I no longer craved sugar.

Amazing!

Something important had occurred in my life. And I wanted to tell others about it so they, too, could experience health benefits.

teaching ZonePerfect healthy eating

After I'd lost body fat and pounds, friends began to ask, "How did you do it?"

My friends had difficulty devising a straightforward system that would keep them eating in a balanced and proportioned way and also fit easily into their hectic schedules. Watching others struggle with weight loss and health and energy issues gave me the idea to create a workshop, so I could help people duplicate my happy results. To my delight, twenty-five people attended my first presentation. Several were health care professionals who began to experience healthy changes. Soon, these health care professionals started sending their patients to me, and my new career as a ZonePerfect instructor began.

I found that the people who came to my classes to learn about ZonePerfect eating wanted to go beyond the current government-approved, food pyramid-view of health. They had tried many other systems, but nothing produced long-lasting results. One of my students made a comment that is typical of those who have attended my classes. She said, "I was getting disgusted with my weight gain. Being on the ZonePerfect program has given me more energy. I'm calmer and I feel I'm on a reversal."

After teaching my class for a couple of years, I met Dr. Paul Kahl, the medical director for ZonePerfect Nutrition. Dr. Kahl attended a tour I was conducting in Austin, Texas at a grocery store that sells natural and organic foods. He suggested that I become a certified ZonePerfect instructor.

The recipes in this cookbook are designed based on the experiences I've gained as a ZonePerfect instructor and through my personal use of the program. From working with thousands of newcomers to the ZonePerfect Nutrition Program, I've found that beginners want something very, very simple. People are choosing to fill their lives with so many things, yet they don't take time to give their bodies the necessary fuel to run efficiently. Starting out by eating simply leads to successfully breaking old habits.

After a couple of weeks, the students in my classes and those I consult with privately get the knack of cooking easy ZonePerfect meals and enjoy moving into more creative recipes. So I've also included some recipes that will take a little more preparation time but yield sensational-tasting results.

All the recipes in this cookbook can be used in meals that follow the ZonePerfect methods of eating balanced portions of proteins, carbohydrates, and fat at each meal. For guidelines on your customized Balanced Portions (from this point on, I'll refer to them as BPs) refer to the ZonePerfect web site at

www.zoneperfect.com.

Go to Getting Started, Resources, and then Body Fat Calculator. On the ZonePerfect web site, you'll also find a list of recommended proteins, fats, and carbohydrates. In the Resources section, go to the Mini Block Guide.

the bigger picture

My goal is to help you fulfill your dreams and your mission in life. I find most people don't have the energy to even think about their dreams, because they're occupied with merely surviving. They go to work and come home at night with just enough energy to take care of the necessities and then go back to work the next day. When I've asked people, including children, to write their goals, they always say that they want more energy. No one feels they have enough energy.

When you begin to eat in the ZonePerfect balanced and proportional way, your cells will be filled with the high quality nutrients, and your body will respond and work more efficiently. You'll finally be free to dream about projects you've always wanted to accomplish and to have the energy to manifest them. With better focus from increased energy, you'll have quality time to spend in any way you want with family, friends, or as a volunteer in your community or church. If you need more energy to succeed at work or sports, you'll have it with the plus factor of clarity in thought and vision.

When I began the ZonePerfect Nutrition Program, for the first time in my life, I felt that losing weight and keeping it off was really possible! I received a heartwarming letter from one of my former students. It reflected my own experiences. She wrote, "I've finally stopped craving sweets. Before this, I was doing things like driving across town to get pastry. Now I exercise every day and I want to. Before your class I was lucky if I walked fifteen minutes a week. On Friday nights I'd usually veg-out on the couch. Last Friday I found myself cleaning my apartment. I had all this energy left over!"

After only one year of using the recipes in this cookbook and eating consistently on the ZonePerfect Nutrition Program, I completed the 26.2-mile Motorola Marathon. Not bad for a former couch potato!

More success is possible than you've ever imagined.

what is the ZonePerfect nutrition program?

The ZonePerfect web site states:

Evolution works very slowly. As far as our genes are concerned, we're still a bunch of hunters/gatherers foraging for food. The problem, of course, is that our genes may be programmed that way, but that's not the way we actually live. We regularly eat large quantities of dense, highly processed carbohydrates, such as grains, and grain-based products, such as pasta. Because we haven't evolved to a stage where we can eat excessive amounts of these high-density carbohydrates without adverse biochemical consequences, our bodies aren't able to operate properly. We gain excess weight, suffer from diabetes, heart disease and a host of other ills, feel sluggish, and generally perform at a sub-par level…

By eating the proper ratio of low-density carbohydrates, dietary fat, and protein, you can control your insulin production. Maintaining your insulin level within a therapeutic zone makes it possible for you to burn excess body fat (and keep it off permanently) and enjoy increased energy, improved mental focus, and increased vitality.

Sounds good to me!

In addition to using the ZonePerfect Nutrition Program, I encourage my clients to find some form of movement they enjoy. Remember, everything in nature moves. And so must you.

One side benefit of adding exercise to your life is how much clearer your ideas become when your brain functions better. I find my ideas are better when I go for a walk than when I lie on the couch and think.

Challenge yourself. There's a whole new level of feeling on top of the world, when you combine eating and cooking on the ZonePerfect plan with exercise.

So how do you begin working the ZonePerfect way of healthful cooking and eating into your daily life?

cooking to suit your lifestyle

If you're like most of the people I've talked with, your schedule varies from busy to insane. This is why I devised three methods that I call your toolbox for fitting the ZonePerfect way of cooking and eating into your schedule.

1 The first method is the "ideal" way. When time permits, chop vegetables, put protein in the oven, and spread favorable fat on your food. There are plenty of recipes in this book that will help you relax and enjoy a good, home-cooked meal.

2 The second method works when your time is more limited. This is when you'll be most tempted to stop for high-carb, fast foods. For those situations I suggest that you have at least five kinds of ready-to-eat proteins in your refrigerator. Most people find it's easy to have high-glycemic carbs on hand. But if you don't want to prepare low-glycemic vegetables and fruit, have packages of these items in your freezer for quick and easy use in the recipes in this book. All you'll need to do then is mix and match proteins with low-glycemic carbohydrates and fat.

3 You'll use the third method of your toolbox when you have no time to prepare an entire meal. Then I suggest using protein powder, add frozen fruit for your carbohydrates, and put in almonds for the fat balance portion. Then mix the ingredients in a blender. Now you're ready to either sit down or jump in the car and make it on time to your next appointment while sipping on a cool, delicious, ZonePerfect smoothie. The ZonePerfect Nutrition Program also offers convenient ready-made products for the ultra busy person, including a complete line of nutrition bars, drinks, and shakes, as well as shelf-stable meals available at www.zoneperfect.com or at grocery and natural food stores.

For a quick reference guide to the three methods in your toolbox (1. When time permits, 2. When time is more limited, and 3. When there's no time to prepare a whole meal), look for the symbols next to each recipe.

omega-3 fish oil

In *Smart Fats, How Dietary Fats and Oils Affect Mental, Physical, and Emotional Intelligence* by Michael A. Schmidt (Frog Ltd., 1997), the author quotes research from Dr. Donald Rudin's book, *The Omega-3 Phenomenon* (Avon, 1988). Dr. Rudin estimates that in the last seventy-five years, people have reduced their Omega-3 fatty acid consumption by 80 percent. Since Omega-3 fatty acids are one of our brain's most vital nutrients, this is alarming.

Dr. Rudin says that we've lost Omega-3 fatty acid in our diets because we're consuming more corn, sunflower, and sesame oils, which are deficient in this element. He also faults the hydrogenation of oils in commercial processing and the fact that we're eating less fish. We're not getting cereal germ in our grain products anymore. He says that we've had a 2500 percent increase in trans-fatty acid intake, and this interferes with fatty acid synthesis. He also blames our loss of Omega-3 fatty acids on a 250 percent increase in sugar consumption, which results in interference with the enzymes of fatty acid synthesis.

Using Omega-3 in your diet improves complexion, increases energy, raises mental alertness, and enhances athletic performance.

You'll want your food to be high in EPA (eicosapentaenoic acid), a fatty acid that is vital to the brain's blood supply. Turn to salmon, sardines, herring, tuna, and mackerel for better sources of EPA. You'll also want to add fish oil supplements that have been molecularly distilled. This process takes out contaminants from the Omega-3. You can get a high-quality Omega-3 supplement at the ZonePerfect website.

Taking these basic ZonePerfect principles and adding the cooking and eating of healthy food brings your nutrition program to a new level of health. In the next section I'll introduce you to a fantastic secret that thousands of others and I have discovered. Combining natural and organic food in cooking with the ZonePerfect nutrition program is tasty, healthy, and benefits all of us, because you're being kind to the earth by using natural ingredients.

why natural and organic foods?

I've spent many years in the natural foods industry and have experienced firsthand the benefits of naturally healthy eating. After mastering the ZonePerfect basics, I began to adapt the program to incorporate natural and organic products into it. I first went to Whole Foods Market to find foods for all the choices in the ZonePerfect way of eating. I wanted to find meat and poultry from free-range, grain-fed animals that contained no added growth hormones, stimulants, antibiotics, nitrates, nitrites, sulfites, artificial preservatives, colorings, or flavorings. In addition, I wanted to eat unprocessed carbohydrates and fruits and vegetables that are certified to be organically grown within a sustainable system of ecological soil management.

I believe that organic foods are superior for improving your health because they don't use synthetic pesticides, fertilizers, or other manufactured chemicals. Even monounsaturated fats, such as olives, olive oil, almond butter, peanut butter, and tahini, can be certified as organic.

I shop at natural food stores because I want to keep my immune system strong. I know that when I go to natural food stores, I don't have to be concerned about food additives, artificial flavors, colors, sweeteners, and synthetic preservatives. Additives break down the immune system, causing allergies and other disease-related conditions.

After devising my system for cooking with natural and organic foods with the ZonePerfect nutritional program, I began teaching classes and individuals how to use it. One of my students wrote, "Kristy Walker's class was a life-changing experience for me as well as for my husband and three children. Not only did I gain a new and more accurate understanding of what real health is but I also have learned how and why to eat healthfully in a super-happy, fat-obsessed, processed, and pre-packaged world."

A mother, who attended my classes, told me she'd started using organic and natural foods to feed her family and discovered that they liked the taste. One night, she was very late and didn't have time to stop at the natural food store on the way home from work to buy ingredients for dinner. Instead she ran to a closer, more convenient store and picked up conventional foods. That evening, her family sat down to eat and immediately asked her why the food tasted so bland. They'd grown to genuinely like natural and organic foods and could tell the difference in freshness and flavor. This mother said that from then on, she always wanted to serve the best food to her family.

I agree with her. And I think you, too, will be delighted by the difference in taste of organic and natural foods.

Organic fruits and vegetables aren't loaded with pesticides. They are produced without the use of toxic pesticides and fertilizers. Organics are processed without artificial ingredients, preservatives, or irradiation.

Organic products support our health, water supply, the environment, and economy. While the rest of the food industry experiments with pesticides, growth hormones, radiation, and genetic engineering, it's nice to know the natural food industry is taking action by going in a healthier direction.

As I was doing research for this topic, I came upon a website you might find interesting: http://www.foodnews.org/. At this site you can shop and put items in your cart which you might normally purchase while cooking and eating such as broccoli, Swiss chard, collards, spinach, apples, salmon, turkey, tomatoes, and rye bread. After you've checked out these items, the site lists all the other elements, i.e. pesticides and chemicals, which you didn't know you were also buying! Doing this exercise may help you to take a closer look at why you'd want to consider switching to organic foods.

The Environmental Working Group has issued "A Shopper's Guide to Pesticides in Produce" which uses information from the U.S. Food and Drug Administration about the amount of pesticides used in forty-two fruits and vegetables. Over half of the total dietary risk from pesticides is concentrated in only twelve crops! The Environmental Protection Agency (EPA) classifies the pesticides in these foods as probably human carcinogens, nervous system poisons, and endocrine system disrupters.

If you aren't able to eat organic fruits and vegetables exclusively, try to avoid the foods on the following list when eating in restaurants. If you are buying non-organic produce from a conventional grocery store always remember to wash it under tap water for thirty seconds before consumption. This will help to reduce most pesticide residue but unfortunately not all.

> **THE MOST PESTICIDE-RIDDEN FOODS, AS LISTED BY THE U.S.F.D.A., ARE:** Strawberries, bell peppers (green and red), spinach, cherries (U.S.), peaches, cantaloupe (Mexican), celery, apples, apricots, green beans, grapes (Chilean), and cucumbers.

Although you can follow the ZonePerfect Nutrition Program without the use of organic and natural foods, why not create the winning combination of ZonePerfect and organic eating? Soon you'll discover, as I did, when you change your way of eating, you bring more balance into your life. As you make positive choices, cooking and eating will become a healthy feast. You'll forget about diets or fads and focus instead on designing and enjoying a yummy, nutritious eating plan for life!

"I don't know how to make vegetables taste good."

"I have always been a meat-and-potato person. The sample foods that Kristy provides in class have broadened my food horizons. I'm now eating things I never would have tried previously. I've learned a much healthier way of eating, and this is now a lifetime habit." —G.H.

"I have changed the way I look at food. Now I view eating more as a way of maintaining fuel rather than as only a pleasurable activity. I am eating lower fat and more whole foods. I've never eaten as many fruits and vegetables." —K.T.

The comments above from students in my classes demonstrate something that I've noticed: Prior to their exposure to the ZonePerfect way of eating and my class, most of them didn't know what to do with vegetables. And they were not familiar with a wide assortment of veggies.

I think that the produce department is one of the most important places in the grocery store. It is where the life is! Many of the recipes in this cookbook are devoted to vegetables.

Vegetarian cookbooks are becoming more popular. More and more people are starting to listen to the child-hood admonition: "Eat your vegetables." Yet most of us don't know much about the wide variety of veggies available or how to cook them so that they taste good. For many people, adding flavor to vegetables means coating them in batter and frying or smothering the little guys in fatty sauces. If you're one of those folks, you're in for a very pleasant surprise when you try some of the delicious vegetable dishes in this cookbook. Vegetables are a pleasing and very flavorful way to create ZonePerfect low-glycemic, carbohydrate-balanced portions and tasty meals.

When I give tours at natural food grocery stores for people who want to learn ZonePerfect principles, I find that most of them have never tried some of the wide variey of greens available. They think of kale as being only for decoration. Swiss chard, bok choy, or Savoy cabbage are as unfamiliar as foreign countries.

In this cookbook you will meet some new friends that will become a welcome part of your ZonePerfect nutrition program and cooking repertoire. If you're like most of my students, you'll be amazed and enlightened by learn-ing about the variety of greens available, what they do for your body, and how to enjoy cooking and eating them.

There are two-dozen types of green vegetables listed in the ZonePerfect food plan's carbohydrate choices. (See http:// www.zoneperfect.com web site for the list.)

This is a lot of vegetables! How many different types of vegetables do you eat in a week?

A friend once said, "Kristy, when you go to the produce department, I want you to buy vegetables that have names you can't pronounce." How strange, I thought. Then I realized that I bought the same vegetables repeatedly. I had tunnel vision. I was choosing a limited diet. No wonder I thought vegetables were boring!

Green, leafy vegetables such as kale, broccoli, cabbage, collard greens, parsley, lettuce, Swiss chard, bok choy, dandelion greens, endive, mustard greens, spinach, sorrel, and cilantro are rich sources of chlorophyll, carotene, calcium, and other vitamins and minerals. Many green, leafy vegetables are part of the cruciferous family of vegetables and contain enzymes that help to protect your body against cancer. Include at least one of these cancer-fighters in your meals each day.

Green, leafy vegetables do so many wonderful things for your body, you're going to begin looking forward to having more of them in your life.

SOME BENEFITS OF EATING GREEN, LEAFY VEGETABLES ARE:

* THEY OFFER PROTECTION AGAINST OSTEOPOROSIS BECAUSE THEY'RE HIGH IN VITAMINS AND MINERALS, SUCH AS CALCIUM. VITAMIN K1 INCREASES BONE DENSITY; AND BORON, A TRACE MINERAL, ASSISTS WITH THE ABSORPTION OF VITAMIN D.

* THEY PROVIDE VITAMIN A IN THE FORM OF CAROTENE, WHICH IS AN ANTI-OXIDANT AND HAS IMMUNE SYSTEM-ENHANCING PROPERTIES.

While I'm giving a grocery store tour, when we get to the frozen food area, I tell my clients to always stock up on a few of the frozen vegetables for easy use in recipes. If you're out of fresh produce, you can use frozen. I recommend Cascadian Farms brand of certified, organic, frozen vegetables. Cascadian Farms harvests no more than 10 minutes from where their vegetables are processed and frozen. The peak nutrition of harvest time isn't lost while produce waits to be processed. Their policy results in great taste. Cascadian Farms green beans, spinach, and broccoli are the best-tasting frozen vegetables I've ever had.

I hope you'll resolve to buy and prepare several green, leafy vegetables each time you shop. And try some new ones too.

In this cookbook you'll find recipes for those who practice vegetarianism or want to get creative with cooking vegetables. These recipes are included throughout the sections for breakfasts, lunches, dinners, and snacks.

When I find myself getting excited about seeing a healthy, robust Swiss chard, I begin wondering if I need to get a life. Then I remember that food is my medicine and energy source. The care I take in selecting food allows me to achieve all my other goals with ease.

Food is something most of us want to enjoy and look forward to eating. Now let me show you how to make ZonePerfect recipes in ways that are simple, quick, and easy to fit into your busy schedule.

keeping it easy

The *American Heritage Dictionary* defines easy as, "capable of being accomplished or acquired with ease; posing no difficulty." When people are first learning the ZonePerfect Nutrition Program, it requires focused attention on remembering that you need protein, carbohydrates, and fat at every meal or snack. If a recipe is complicated, I find that people feel this is too much for them. However, if the recipe requires very few ingredients and just mixing and matching them, then it seems much easier.

The recipes in this cookbook are the ones that I work with everyday. I like very simple eating and I want it to taste good but not take a lot of time. People tell me that they love the taste of the ingredients I use in my recipes. I flavor foods with a product called Spike, which can be found at most natural food stores. It is a combination of vegetables and herb spices and is great on just about everything.

All of the recipes in this cookbook are quick to prepare. You'll cut down on prep time by keeping your refrigerator well-stocked with food. Because I shop only once a week, if my vegetable crisper is hard to open after putting the groceries away, then I know I have enough vegetables.

I suggest that you keep in the fridge five different proteins that are ready to eat. This will make it possible for you to not have to cook proteins for every meal. I keep fish and turkey burgers in the freezer.

Also, keep five different fruits on hand. Stock up on frozen vegetables too. The more items on the ZonePerfect food lists that you have in your refrigerator, the easier it is to stay on the Program and you will be able to put together meals almost effortlessly.

I have some clients that plan all their meals for the week. I'm not that organized. As long as I have all the ingredients stocked, I pull them out in a moment and mix, match, and enjoy.

I've heard it said that people have twenty meals they regularly eat and repeat. I find this is true for me. The easy meals are ones that I repeat. I use different proteins, vegetables, and fruits for variety.

K.I.S.S. rule

Below are some tried and true methods I've found for making ZonePerfect food preparation simple.

HAVE 3 SETS OF MEASURING SPOONS READILY AVAILABLE. If you only have one set, you will find that you are constantly looking for it. And it's always in the dishwasher or somewhere else when you need it.

ALWAYS KEEP MEASURING SCOOPS OUT ON YOUR COUNTER. I keep mine in a basket on the counter because I use them daily to measure fruits, veggies, and cottage cheese, etc.

A FOOD SCALE IS A CRITICAL TOOL. When I first realized I needed to get a food scale, I had quite an attitude about this. However, the more I used the food scale, the better idea I had of what amount of foods I was supposed to be eating. Soon, whenever I went out to eat, because I'd used the food scale so often, I could tell by sight how large a portion I was supposed to have.

A VEGETABLE STEAMER HELPS TO RETAIN THE ENZYMES IN YOUR VEGETABLES. Plus, cooking in the steamer is fast, and you can put three carbohydrate BPs in it at one time. This makes for fast and healthy cooking.

YOU NEED A SHARP KNIFE. If your knife is even a little dull, you will find that you don't want to cut up produce. A sharp knife saves you a lot of cooking time.

KEEP A CUTTING BOARD OUT ON THE COUNTER. You will use it every day.

ALWAYS HAVE FIVE TYPES OF READY-TO-EAT ZONEPERFECT PROTEINS IN THE FRIDGE. If you don't feel like cooking, you can use them.

KEEP FROZEN FRUIT IN THE FREEZER. If you run out of other choices before your next trip to the grocery store, you can always make a quick smoothie.

HAVE FROZEN VEGETABLES IN YOUR FREEZER. If you are out of fresh veggies, then you will always have in stock incredible tasting, precut veggies that are ready to go.

BUY A PACK OF BOTTLED WATER AND KEEP IT IN YOUR CAR. You will be amazed at how much more water you will drink.

YOU WILL WANT TO SUPPLEMENT YOUR DIET WITH OMEGA-3 FISH OIL.

ZONEPERFECT BARS ARE EASY TO CARRY WITH YOU WHEN YOU TRAVEL.

Are you ready now to join me on an eating and nutritional adventure? As you try the recipes in this cookbook, know that you are gaining health and energy. Your weight loss goals are closer with every ZonePerfect meal.

ZonePerfect breakfasts

table of contents:

raspberry and blueberry smoothie

4 oz water
1 cup fresh or frozen raspberries
1 cup fresh or frozen blueberries
3 scoops ZonePerfect Protein Powder (21 grams)
4 1/2 tsp slivered almonds

If using fresh raspberries and blueberries, rinse well.

Put all ingredients in blender and blend until smooth.

Pour into glass and enjoy.

3 Protein BPs
3 Carbohydrate BPs
3 Fat BPs

CODE TOOL CHEST
#3

apricot almond smoothie

4 oz water

3 fresh apricots, pitted and chopped

4 1/2 tsp slivered almonds

1 tsp vanilla extract

3 scoops ZonePerfect Protein Powder (21 grams)

Put water, apricots, almonds, vanilla, and protein powder in blender. Blend until smooth. Pour into glass.

3 Protein BPs

3 Carbohydrate BPs

3 Fat BPs

CODE TOOL CHEST

#3

cherry and blueberry smoothie

4 oz water

3/4 cup frozen cherries

1 cup frozen blueberries

3 scoops ZonePerfect Protein Powder (21 grams)

4 1/2 tsp slivered almonds

Put all ingredients in blender and blend until smooth. Pour into glass and enjoy.

3 Protein BPs

3 Carbohydrate BPs

3 Fat BPs

CODE TOOL CHEST

#3

blackberry and cherry smoothie

4 oz water
3/4 cup frozen blackberries
3/4 cup frozen cherries
2 scoops ZonePerfect Protein Powder (14 grams)
7 grams spirulina (available at most natural food stores)*
4 1/2 tsp slivered almonds

*This smoothie can be made without the spirulina.
Just add another scoop of the ZonePerfect Protein Powder
to get your 3 portions of protein.

Put all ingredients in blender and blend until smooth. Pour into glass.

3 Protein BPs
3 Carbohydrate BPs
3 Fat BPs

CODE TOOL CHEST

strawberry swirl smoothie

4 oz water
2 cups frozen or fresh strawberries
3 scoops ZonePerfect Protein Powder (21 grams)
1/2 slice 100% rye bread, toasted
1 tsp almond butter

If using fresh strawberries, wash well. Put water, strawberries, and protein powder in blender. Blend until smooth. Pour into glass.

Toast rye bread. Spread toast with almond butter. Serve with smoothie.

This recipe gives you something to drink and something to chew!

3 Protein BPs
3 Carbohydrate BPs
3 Fat BPs

CODE TOOL CHEST
#3

Tip: This simple recipe can be changed by substituting the strawberries for 2 cups raspberries or 1 1/2 cups cherries or 1 cup blueberries or 1 cup fresh pineapple.

strawberry yogurt delight smoothie

4 oz water

1 cup strawberries, washed

1 cup plain yogurt

1 scoop ZonePerfect Protein Powder (7 grams)

1 tsp flaxseed oil or 4 1/2 tsp slivered almonds

Put all ingredients into blender. Blend until smooth. Pour into glass and enjoy.

3 Protein BPs

3 Carbohydrate BPs

3 Fat BPs

CODE TOOL CHEST

#3

tropical breakfast smoothie

1/2 cup water
1/2 cup plain yogurt
1 cup pineapple chunks, cubed
2 scoops ZonePerfect Protein Powder (14 grams)
3 Macadamia nuts, chopped or crushed
1 mint sprig

Blend together water, yogurt, pineapple, and protein powder in a blender until smooth.
Pour into glass. Garnish with macadamia nuts and a mint sprig.

3 Protein BPs
3 Carbohydrate BPs
3 Fat BPs

CODE TOOL CHEST
#3

berry cherry smoothie

4 oz water
3 scoops ZonePerfect Protein Powder (21 grams)
1 cup fresh or frozen strawberries
3/4 cup fresh or frozen cherries
1/2 piece 100% rye bread, toasted
1 tsp almond butter

If using fresh strawberries and cherries, wash well first. Put 4 oz water in blender and add protein powder, strawberries, and cherries. Blend until smooth.

Toast rye bread and spread with almond butter.

Pour smoothie in a glass and enjoy with toast.

3 Protein BPs
3 Carbohydrate BPs
3 Fat BPs

CODE TOOL CHEST
#3

easy cottage cheese and cantaloupe delight

3/4 cup low-fat cottage cheese
3/4 cup cantaloupe, cubed
3 macadamia nuts, chopped or crushed
1 piece 100% rye bread, toasted

Mix cantaloupe into the cottage cheese. Top with crushed nuts and enjoy with a piece of delicious rye toast.

3 Protein BPs
3 Carbohydrate BPs
3 Fat BPs

CODE TOOL CHEST
#3

ever-so-easy cottage cheese and fruit delight

3/4 cup low-fat cottage cheese
1/2 cup fresh pineapple chunks
1/2 apple, sliced
1 cup strawberries
4 1/2 tsp slivered almonds

Put cottage cheese in bowl. Add fruit. Add nuts. Enjoy.
This can be eaten for breakfast, lunch, or dinner!

3 Protein BPs
3 Carbohydrate BPs
3 Fat BPs

CODE TOOL CHEST
#3

apple, almond, and ricotta on rye with turkey bacon

3 strips turkey bacon
1/2 cup skim ricotta cheese
1/2 apple, finely chopped or grated
9 almonds, toasted and chopped
cinnamon, to taste
1 piece rye bread, toasted

Cook the turkey bacon in a nonstick skillet on medium-high heat. While the bacon is cooking, mix the ricotta cheese with apples and almonds. Add cinnamon to taste, if desired. Spoon this mixture over rye toast. Serve with turkey bacon.

3 Protein BPs
3 Carbohydrate BPs
3 Fat BPs

CODE TOOL CHEST
#2

yogurt with strawberries

1 cup plain yogurt
1 scoop ZonePerfect Protein Powder (7 grams)
1/2 tsp almond extract
1 cup fresh strawberries, washed
4 1/2 tsp slivered almonds

Place 1 cup plain yogurt in a serving bowl. Stir in protein powder and almond extract.
Add strawberries. Sprinkle with almonds.

3 Protein BPs
3 Carbohydrate BPs
3 Fat BPs

CODE TOOL CHEST
#3

apple cinnamon oats

1/4 cup steel-cut oats
1/3 cup unsweetened apple sauce
cinnamon
3 scoops ZonePerfect Protein Powder (21 grams)
4 1/2 tsp almonds, sliced

Bring 1 1/2 cups water to a rolling boil. Add steel-cut oats. Simmer on low heat for 15 to 20 minutes. Stir in apple sauce. Sprinkle cinnamon on top.

Put protein powder in bowl and then pour oatmeal/apple cinnamon sauce mixture over the top. Stir with a fork. If the mixture is too thick, add more water. Sprinkle almonds on top.

3 Protein BPs
3 Carbohydrate BPs
3 Fat BPs

CODE TOOL CHEST
#3

cheerie oats

1/4 cup steel-cut oats
3/4 cup frozen or fresh cherries
cinnamon
3 scoops of ZonePerfect Protein Powder (21 grams)
4 1/2 tsp slivered almonds

If using fresh cherries, wash well. Bring 1 1/2 cups water to a rolling boil. Add steel cut oats. Simmer on low heat for 15 to 20 minutes. Add cherries while oatmeal is cooking. Sprinkle cinnamon on oatmeal and cherries. Put protein powder in bowl, pour in the oatmeal/cherry mixture and stir with a fork. If the mixture is too thick, add more water. Sprinkle chopped almonds on top.

3 Protein BPs
3 Carbohydrate BPs
3 Fat BPs

CODE TOOL CHEST
#3

fruit in season oatmeal

1/4 cup steel-cut oats
3 scoops ZonePerfect Protein Powder (21 grams)
cinnamon
1 cup fresh strawberries, washed or 1 peach, peeled
    or 1/2 cup blueberries, washed
4 1/2 tsp slivered almonds

Bring 1 1/2 cups water to a rolling boil. Add steel-cut oats. Simmer on low heat for 15 to 20 minutes. Put protein powder in bowl. Pour in cooked oatmeal. Stir with a fork. If mixture is too thick, add more water. Sprinkle cinnamon on oatmeal. Add fresh fruit from the choices listed above. Sprinkle almonds on top.

3 Protein BPs
3 Carbohydrate BPs
3 Fat BPs

CODE TOOL CHEST

#2

oatmeal with applesauce and yogurt

1/3 cup steel-cut oats, cooked
1/2 cup plain yogurt
1/3 cup unsweetened applesauce
1 tb walnuts, chopped
2 oz turkey sausage, prepared

Top cooked oatmeal with yogurt, then applesauce. Sprinkle walnuts on top. Serve with turkey sausage.

3 Protein BPs
3 Carbohydrate BPs
3 Fat BPs

CODE TOOL CHEST
#2

peachy oatmeal with peanuts

1/4 cup steel-cut oats
1 ripe peach, peeled, if desired, and chopped
18 peanuts
cinnamon and nutmeg, to taste, if desired
3/4 cup low-fat cottage cheese

Bring 1 1/2 cups of water to a rolling boil. Add steel-cut oats. Simmer on low heat for 15 to 20 minutes. Pour cooked oatmeal into serving bowl. Mix cooked oatmeal with chopped peach. Add peanuts. Top with cinnamon and nutmeg, if desired. Serve with cottage cheese.

3 Protein BPs
3 Carbohydrate BPs
3 Fat BPs

CODE TOOL CHEST
#2

mixed fruits with oatmeal and yogurt

1/3 cup steel-cut oats cooked
1/2 cup plain yogurt
1/2 cup raspberries, washed
1/4 cup blueberries, washed
4 1/2 tsp slivered almonds
1/2 tsp ground cinnamon, for garnish
2 oz turkey sausage, cooked

Pour cooked oatmeal into serving bowl. Top cooked oatmeal with yogurt, fruit, and almonds.
Sprinkle with cinnamon. Serve with cooked turkey sausage.

3 Protein BPs
3 Carbohydrate BPs
3 Fat BPs

CODE TOOL CHEST
#2

italian egg white scramble

nonstick cooking spray
1/2 cup zucchini, grated
6 medium cherry tomatoes, washed and cut in half
4 egg whites
2 tb grated Parmesan cheese
1 tb fresh basil leaves, chopped
1/4 tsp dried thyme
salt and pepper
1 slice 100% rye bread, toasted
1 tsp olive oil

Heat skillet on medium. Spray with nonstick cooking spray. Add zucchini and tomatoes and sauté. Beat egg whites until frothy. Slowly pour over sautéed tomatoes and zucchini, then cook, stirring until eggs are set. Sprinkle with the grated Parmesan cheese and fresh and dried herbs. Add salt and pepper, to taste. Drizzle olive oil over rye toast. Serve immediately.

3 Protein BPs
3 Carbohydrate BPs
3 Fat BPs

CODE TOOL CHEST
#1

blueberry almond toast with turkey sausage

nonstick cooking spray
2 oz turkey sausage
1/2 piece 100% rye bread
1 tsp almond butter
1/2 cup blueberries, divided
1/2 cup plain yogurt

Brown sausage in skillet sprayed with nonstick cooking spray. Cook until done. While sausage cooks, toast rye bread and spread with almond butter. Top almond butter toast with 1/4 cup blueberries. Mix remaining 1/4 cup blueberries into yogurt. Serve with hot, cooked turkey sausage.

3 Protein BPs
3 Carbohydrate BPs
3 Fat BPs

CODE TOOL CHEST
#2

bacon and egg whites

nonstick cooking spray
1 oz Canadian-style bacon
4 egg whites
1 slice 100% rye bread
1 tsp almond butter
2/3 cup honeydew melon
salt and pepper, to taste

Spray a skillet with nonstick cooking spray. Add Canadian-style bacon to skillet and cook on medium-high heat until browned. Beat egg whites. Add to bacon while it is cooking. Cook eggs and bacon, stirring, until set. As eggs are cooking, toast rye bread. Spread almond butter on toast. Arrange fruit on plate with eggs, bacon, and toast.

3 Protein BPs
3 Carbohydrate BPs
3 Fat BPs

CODE TOOL CHEST
#2

scrambled egg whites with turkey sausage

nonstick cooking spray
2 oz turkey sausage
2 egg whites
Spike seasoning
1 slice 100% rye bread
3 tb avocado
2/3 cup honeydew melon

Cut turkey sausage into bite-size pieces. Spray nonstick cooking spray in a small frying pan. Add turkey sausage to pan. Heat on medium-high until cooked through and browned. Add egg whites to heated pan with sausage and cook, stirring until eggs are set. Sprinkle with Spike seasoning. Toast rye bread and spread avocado on toast. Arrange on plate with scrambled eggs, turkey sausage, and honeydew melon.

3 Protein BPs
3 Carbohydrate BPs
3 Fat BPs

CODE TOOL CHEST
#2

Kristy says: Many stores sell pre-cut pineapple, cantaloupe, and honeydew melon.
This is a time-saver. All you have to do is scoop and eat.

eggs with smoked salmon on rye

2 tb light cream cheese (Neufchâtel)
1 slice 100% rye toast
1 egg
2 egg whites
nonstick cooking spray
1 1/2 oz smoked salmon, sliced into bite-size pieces
salt and pepper, to taste
1/2 cup pineapple chunks

Spread light cream cheese on top of rye toast and set aside. Blend egg with egg whites in a small bowl. Spray a nonstick skillet with nonstick cooking spray. Add eggs and scramble gently. When nearly cooked, add smoked salmon. When eggs are cooked to your liking, spoon on top of cream cheese and toast. Serve with pineapple chunks on the side.

3 Protein BPs
3 Carbohydrate BPs
3 Fat BPs

CODE TOOL CHEST

#2

scrambled spinach, feta, and egg whites

nonstick cooking spray
1 tb onions, sliced
4 cups baby spinach leaves
2 egg whites
2 oz feta cheese
1 piece 100% rye bread
1 tsp olive oil
3/4 cup cantaloupe
salt and pepper or Spike seasoning, to taste

Spray pan with a touch of nonstick cooking spray and heat on medium. Add onions and cook until translucent. Add baby spinach leaves and cook until tender. Add egg whites and feta cheese to onions and spinach and cook, stirring until eggs are set. Toast rye bread and drizzle with 1 tsp of olive oil.

Cut cantaloupe and arrange on plate with toast and scrambled egg with feta. Sprinkle Spike seasoning or salt and pepper, to taste.

Tip: The onions and spinach leaves are free with no BPs counted, due to the small amount.

3 Protein BPs
3 Carbohydrate BPs
3 Fat BPs

CODE TOOL CHEST

chive scrambled tofu with tomatoes, mozzarella, and grapes

1/2 cup onion, chopped
1 tsp olive oil
4 oz firm tofu, crumbled
1 tb chives, freshly snipped
salt, pepper, or a dash of tamari, to taste
1/8 tsp turmeric powder
1 oz mozzarella cheese, grated
1 red, ripe tomato, washed and sliced
1 cup red or green grapes, washed

Sauté onion in olive oil in a nonstick pan over medium heat for 5 minutes, stirring frequently. Add crumbled tofu, chives, and seasonings. Stir well to coat tofu. Add turmeric for a natural yellow color, similar to egg yolk. Cook until very hot. Sprinkle cheese over tofu and allow it to melt. Serve tofu spooned over sliced tomatoes with grapes on the side.

3 Protein BPs
3 Carbohydrate BPs
3 Fat BPs

CODE TOOL CHEST
#1

sunday mushroom and green pepper frittata

nonstick cooking spray
1/2 cup green peppers, washed and chopped
1 cup mushrooms, wiped clean and chopped
salt, pepper, and dried oregano, to taste
2 eggs
2 egg whites
1/2 piece 100% rye bread, toasted
1 1/2 tsp sesame tahini
1/2 cup strawberries, washed
1/2 cup blueberries, washed

Spray nonstick cooking spray in small skillet. Sauté green peppers and mushrooms over medium-high heat for about 10 minutes or until mushrooms give up their juices. Season to taste with salt, pepper, and oregano.

In a separate bowl, beat together the eggs and egg whites. Add beaten eggs to skillet. Season again, if desired. Cook until eggs are set. Serve with rye toast, topped with sesame tahini, and strawberries and blueberries on the side.

3 Protein BPs
3 Carbohydrate BPs
3 Fat BPs

CODE TOOL CHEST
#1

scrambled mexican tofu

6 oz smoked tofu, firm
nonstick cooking spray
1/2 cup salsa
1/4 cup black beans, cooked
1/2 slice 100% rye bread, toasted
3 tb avocado

Cut tofu into bite-size pieces. Spray nonstick cooking spray in small frying pan. Add salsa, black beans, and tofu. Cook on medium heat for 5 to 8 minutes or until heated thoroughly. Spread avocado on toast. Ole!

3 Protein BPs
3 Carbohydrate BPs
3 Fat BPs

CODE TOOL CHEST

#2

poached egg whites with feta surprise

2 egg whites
2 oz feta cheese
1 piece 100% rye bread
1 cup fresh strawberries, washed, or 3/4 cup cantaloupe
3 tb avocado

Place each egg white into an individual egg poacher cup over simmering water. Add 1 oz feta cheese into each poacher cup with egg whites. Put toast in toaster. Cut fruit and put on plate. After egg whites have cooked, scoop out and add to plate with fruit. Spread avocado on toast. Enjoy!

3 Protein BPs
3 Carbohydrate BPs
3 Fat BPs

CODE TOOL CHEST

#2

greek omelet with fresh herbs

1 tsp olive oil, divided
1/2 cup cherry tomatoes, cut in half
1/2 cup onions, chopped
2 eggs, beaten
salt and pepper, to taste
1 oz feta cheese
1 to 2 tb fresh oregano leaves
1 tb fresh basil leaves, slivered
2 ripe kiwi fruit, peeled and sliced

In a nonstick omelet skillet on medium heat, sauté tomatoes and onions in 1/2 tsp olive oil for 4 to 5 minutes. Set aside in a bowl. Add the remaining 1/2 tsp oil to the pan. Add beaten eggs and cook, stirring, until set. Season to taste with salt and pepper. When eggs are cooked, top with sautéed veggies, feta cheese, and fresh herbs. Fold over to make an omelet. Serve with sliced kiwi.

3 Protein BPs
3 Carbohydrate BPs
3 Fat BPs

CODE TOOL CHEST
#1

ZonePerfect
lunches

table of contents:

beef with bok choy and cucumber salad

nonstick cooking spray
3 oz lean beef
freshly ground black pepper
3 cups bok choy
2 cups cucumber, sliced
8 cherry tomatoes, sliced
1/4 cup pineapple, cubed
bed of mixed lettuce, washed
3 tb low-fat peanut sauce

Spray nonstick spray in skillet. Heat skillet medium-high. Grind coarse black pepper on both sides of beef. Sear beef on each side until cooked to your preference. Rinse and dry bok choy, chop leaves into bite-size pieces, and steam. While bok choy is steaming, lay cucumber and tomato slices over bed of mixed lettuce greens. Top with pineapple, beef, and bok choy. Pour peanut sauce over entire salad.

3 Protein BPs
3 Carbohydrate BPs
3 Fat BPs

CODE TOOL CHEST

#1

crunchy tofu curry salad

1 1/2 cups leafy green lettuce, torn into bite-size pieces
1/2 cup red pepper, washed and cut in strips
1/4 cup black beans
1/2 cup pineapple, cubed
1 tsp extra virgin olive oil
1 tsp lemon juice, or to taste
4 oz savory baked tofu, chopped into bite-size pieces
2 tb non-fat chicken broth
1/8 tsp curry powder, or to taste
1/2 cup non-fat plain yogurt

Mix the lettuce, red pepper, black beans, and pineapple together in a bowl. Toss with olive oil and lemon juice. Set aside.

In a nonstick skillet, sauté tofu in chicken broth seasoned with curry powder until very hot. Adjust seasonings to personal taste. Immediately spoon the curry tofu on top of the salad. Serve topped with yogurt.

3 Protein BPs
3 Carbohydrate BPs
3 Fat BPs

CODE TOOL CHEST

#2

orange chicken and snow pea salad

nonstick cooking spray
3 oz breast of chicken
freshly ground black pepper
1 1/2 cups snow peas, washed
1 cup radicchio, washed
1 orange
2 cups salad greens, washed
3 tb avocado chunks
2 tb balsamic vinegar

Spray skillet with nonstick spray. Heat skillet on medium-high heat. Grind fresh black pepper on one side of chicken breast. Lay the chicken, pepper-side-down, on the skillet. Coat top side of chicken with pepper. Cook approximately 4 minutes per side until no longer pink in the center.

While chicken is cooking, trim ends of snow peas. Tear radicchio into bite-size pieces. Peel and section orange. Arrange salad greens and radicchio on plate. Steam snow peas for 1 minute.

When chicken is cooked, serve on top of salad greens. Garnish with snow peas, orange sections, and avocado. Sprinkle balsamic vinegar over salad.

3 Protein BPs
3 Carbohydrate BPs
3 Fat BPs

CODE TOOL CHEST

#1

salmon and feta salad

3 cups salad greens, washed
3 oz salmon, smoked or cooked
1 oz feta cheese
1 cup green beans, washed and steamed
1/2 apple, sliced into small pieces
1/2 lemon, squeezed onto apples
2 tomatoes, washed and sliced
1 tb raspberry vinegar
1 tsp olive oil
Spike seasoning or lemon pepper (optional)
1 tsp fresh dill, chopped

Arrange lettuce mixture on plate. Cut salmon in bite-size pieces and add on top of lettuce mixture. Crumble feta cheese on top of salad. Add green beans, apple, and tomatoes. Whisk together oil and vinegar. Pour vinaigrette on top of salmon salad and sprinkle with Spike or lemon pepper seasoning, if desired. Garnish with dill.

3 Protein BPs
3 Carbohydrate BPs
3 Fat BPs

CODE TOOL CHEST
#2

smoked trout pear salad

1/4 tsp shallot
1/4 tsp white miso
1 tsp water
1 tb raspberry vinegar
1 tsp champagne mustard
1 ripe fig
4 cups mixed salad greens, washed
1/2 Asian pear, washed and cored, sliced
8 yellow pear tomatoes or cherry tomatoes, washed
3 oz smoked trout
1 oz feta cheese, crumbled
9 pecans

Peel and mince shallot. In a mixing bowl whisk together miso, water, shallot, raspberry vinegar, and mustard. Quarter fig. Place mixed baby greens on salad plate. Layer with pear, tomatoes, smoked trout, feta cheese, and fig. Drizzle dressing on top. Garnish with pecans.

3 Protein BPs
3 Carbohydrate BPs
3 Fat BPs

CODE TOOL CHEST
#2

sautéed shrimp on arugula and white bean salad

3 cups arugula greens, washed, stems trimmed and patted dry
8 cherry tomatoes, washed and sliced in half
1/2 cup canned chickpeas, rinsed and drained
1 tsp olive oil
1 tb red wine vinegar
1 tsp fresh rosemary or 1/8 tsp dried
1 clove garlic, minced
nonstick cooking spray
4 1/2 oz fresh shrimp, cleaned and deveined
1 tb lemon juice
salt and pepper, to taste

Arrange arugula, cherry tomatoes, and chickpeas on salad plate. Whisk together olive oil, vinegar, rosemary, and garlic. Season with salt and pepper then set aside while preparing shrimp.

Heat nonstick skillet to medium heat. Spray skillet with nonstick cooking spray. Add shrimp and lemon juice and sauté for 5 minutes or until shrimp turns bright pink. Add salt and pepper, to taste. Arrange sautéed shrimp on top of salad and drizzle with olive oil mixture. Serve immediately.

3 Protein BPs
3 Carbohydrate BPs
3 Fat BPs

CODE TOOL CHEST
#1

trout and pineapple salad

3 cups bok choy leaves
2 cups yellow squash
4 cups salad greens, washed
4 1/2 oz smoked trout
1/2 cup fresh pineapple, cubed
1 tb red wine vinegar
1 tsp olive oil
1 tsp fresh ginger, minced
1 tsp garlic, minced
Spike or herb seasoning (optional)

Wash and cut bok choy and yellow squash into bite-size pieces. Steam together in vegetable steamer. Arrange lettuce mixture on plate. Cut trout in bite-size pieces. Add to salad with steamed bok choy and squash. Add cubed pineapple. Mix together vinegar, oil, fresh ginger, and garlic. Drizzle over top of salad. Add Spike or mixed herb seasoning, if desired.

3 Protein BPs
3 Carbohydrate BPs
3 Fat BPs

CODE TOOL CHEST

#2

tuna and carrot salad

2 cups zucchini
1 cup green beans
3 cups salad greens, washed
1/2 carrot, peeled
3 oz water-packed tuna, drained
1 tsp fresh dill, chopped
1 scallion, diced
juice of 1/2 lemon
1 tsp olive oil

Wash and slice zucchini into half-moons and green beans into one-inch pieces. Steam zucchini and green beans until tender. Arrange salad greens on plate. Grate carrot and add to salad mixture. Place steamed zucchini and green beans over salad. Add tuna. Sprinkle chopped dill and scallion over salad. Squeeze lemon juice over salad, drizzle with olive oil, and serve.

3 Protein BPs
3 Carbohydrate BPs
3 Fat BPs

CODE TOOL CHEST
#2

tangerine shrimp salad with avocado dressing

3 oz shrimp
1 cup green beans
mixture of baby field greens, washed
1 1/2 cups artichoke hearts, packed in water
1 tangerine, peeled and sectioned
1 oz goat cheese
1 clove garlic, minced
1 tb red wine vinegar
3 tb avocado
2 tb tomato juice (fresh or canned)
1/2 tsp minced chervil

Peel, de-vein, and steam shrimp until pink. Wash and steam green beans until tender. Arrange salad greens on plate and add shrimp, green beans, artichoke hearts, and tangerine sections. Crumble goat cheese over salad. Purée garlic, vinegar, avocado, and tomato juice in a blender to make a dressing. Add chervil to dressing. Drizzle dressing over salad.

3 Protein BPs
3 Carbohydrate BPs
3 Fat BPs

CODE TOOL CHEST
#1

tuna apple salad – stuffed tomato

2 firm, ripe red tomatoes, washed
3 oz canned water-packed albacore tuna, drained
1/4 cup green onion, chopped
1/2 cup plus 2 tb chopped celery
1/2 apple, cored and chopped (peeled, if desired)
1 tb natural light mayonnaise (Spectrum Light Canola Mayo or Nasoya Nayonnaise)
salt and pepper, to taste
1 cup green beans, steamed to crispy tender

Cut tops off tomatoes. Using a sharp knife and a soup spoon, gently cut around and scoop out the insides of the tomatoes, leaving two "tomato bowls." Set aside. Chop flesh from tomato tops and insides, discarding seeds. Place in a bowl. Add tuna, onion, celery, apple, and mayo. Season to taste with salt and pepper. Stuff the 2 tomatoes with tuna-apple mixture. Serve surrounded with green beans.

3 Protein BPs
3 Carbohydrate BPs
3 Fat BPs

CODE TOOL CHEST

venison, green bean, and tomato feta salad

nonstick cooking spray
2 oz venison
2 cups green or red bell pepper, cut into strips
black pepper, to taste
1 cup green beans, washed and trimmed
1 tb balsamic vinegar
1 tsp olive oil
1/2 tsp minced ginger
1 clove minced garlic
1 tsp minced chives
1 tb water
1 tsp prepared coarse ground mustard
mixed bed of lettuce, washed
2 tomatoes, washed and sliced
1 oz feta cheese

Spray skillet with nonstick cooking spray. Cube venison into bite-size pieces. Cook venison in skillet on medium-high heat with bell peppers and black pepper, to taste. Steam green beans. In small bowl whisk together vinegar, oil, ginger, garlic, chives, water, and mustard. Arrange salad mixture on plate and add sliced tomatoes, green beans, venison, and bell peppers. Crumble feta and add to salad. Drizzle with salad dressing.

3 Protein BPs
3 Carbohydrate BPs
3 Fat BPs

CODE TOOL CHEST
#1

shaved ham, melon, and goat cheese salad

4 cups arugula
2 tb orange juice, freshly-squeezed
1 tb raspberry vinegar
1 tsp olive oil
black pepper and salt, to taste
1 1/2 cups cantaloupe, cubed
2 oz lean ham, thinly sliced
1 oz goat cheese
3 Finn Crisp rye crackers

Wash and drain arugula and trim stem ends. Pat dry with a towel. Tear into bite-size pieces.

To make the dressing, mix together freshly-squeezed orange juice, vinegar, and olive oil. Season with salt and pepper, to taste. Spread arugula, cantaloupe, and shaved ham on a salad plate. Sprinkle with goat cheese. Drizzle the dressing over the salad and serve with crackers.

3 Protein BPs
3 Carbohydrate BPs
3 Fat BPs

CODE TOOL CHEST
#2

bacon, lettuce, and cheese sandwich

2 oz Canadian-style bacon
1 slice 100% rye bread
3 tb avocado
lettuce
one slice tomato
1 oz low-fat cheese
mustard (optional)
1/2 apple

Heat Canadian-style bacon. Cut bread in half and toast. Spread avocado on one-half of toast. Cut Canadian-style bacon to fit on bread. Add lettuce, tomato, and cheese. Add mustard, if desired. Top with other slice of toast. Place on the plate with apple on side.

(This is also good when grilled as a hot sandwich.)

3 Protein BPs
3 Carbohydrate BPs
3 Fat BPs

CODE TOOL CHEST

#2

shrimp tacos

4 oz shrimp, fresh or already cooked
2 corn tortillas
1 cup lettuce, washed and shredded
3 tb ripe avocado
1/2 cup purple cabbage, shredded
1/2 lime
1/4 cup plain yogurt
1/4 cup salsa
1 tsp prepared horseradish (optional)

If using fresh shrimp, peel, de-vein, and boil until bright pink. Wrap tortillas in foil and heat in oven until warm. Fill each tortilla with equal amounts of shrimp, lettuce, avocado, and cabbage. Squeeze lime into yogurt and stir. Drizzle one-half yogurt mixture and one-half salsa with added horseradish, if desired, into each tortilla. Serve immediately.

3 Protein BPs
3 Carbohydrate BPs
3 Fat BPs

CODE TOOL CHEST
#1

mexican fish taco

4 1/2 oz orange roughy or salmon
salt and pepper, to taste
1 tb lemon juice
nonstick cooking spray
1/2 stalk celery, washed and diced
1/2 cup yellow bell pepper, washed and diced
1/2 cup onion, diced
2 corn tortillas
3 tb ripe avocado
1 tomato, washed and chopped
3 sprigs fresh cilantro, chopped

Cut the fish into bite-size pieces. Season with salt, pepper, and lemon juice. Heat sauté pan on medium. Spray with light mist of nonstick spray. Sauté celery, yellow pepper, and onion for 2 minutes. Arrange on one side of sauté pan. Add fish and sauté for approximately 2 to 3 minutes per side or until fish turns opaque. Wrap two tortillas in foil and place in oven for 5 minutes. Add one-half of the fish and one-half of the remaining ingredients to each heated tortilla. Roll up and enjoy! Serve hot.

3 Protein BPs
3 Carbohydrate BPs
3 Fat BPs

CODE TOOL CHEST
#1

smoked trout and feta sandwich

1 slice 100% rye bread
3 tb ripe avocado
3 oz smoked trout
1 oz feta cheese
1/2 apple

Toast bread. Spread with avocado. Place smoked trout on toast. Sprinkle with feta
and put in toaster oven until heated. Add lettuce, if desired.

3 Protein BPs
3 Carbohydrate BPs
3 Fat BPs

easy open-faced turkey sandwich

1 slice 100% rye bread
3 tb ripe avocado
4 1/2 oz deli turkey
mixed baby greens, washed (optional)
1/2 apple

Toast rye bread. Spread avocado on toast. Put turkey on top of bread as an open-faced sandwich. For fun
(and health), you can add a salad mixture of different kinds of lettuce leaves. Serve with apple on the side.

3 Protein BPs
3 Carbohydrate BPs
3 Fat BPs

tuna melt sandwich

1 slice 100% rye bread
2 oz water-packed tuna, drained
1 tomato, washed and sliced horizontally
1 oz low-fat cheddar cheese
1/4 cup red onion, thinly sliced
3 cups salad greens, washed
1 tsp olive oil
1 tb vinegar
salt and pepper, to taste

Arrange tuna and one slice of tomato on rye bread. Place onion, then cheese slice on top of tuna. Toast in toaster oven or under broiler until cheese melts. Serve hot with side salad of mixed greens and remaining tomato slices drizzled with olive oil and vinegar. Season to taste with salt and pepper.

3 Protein BPs
3 Carbohydrate BPs
3 Fat BPs

CODE TOOL CHEST
#2

Kristy says: "All types of salad greens are considered free Balanced Portions as they have such a small amount of carbohydrate grams per ounce. So, eat up!"

simple chicken sandwich

1 slice 100% whole wheat bread
3 tb ripe avocado
3 oz chicken, cooked
lettuce leaves or sprouts, washed
1 tangerine

Toast the bread. Spread toast with avocado. Put chicken on top of bread as an open-faced sandwich.
Top with lettuce leaves or sprouts. Enjoy with a tangerine.

3 Protein BPs
3 Carbohydrate BPs
3 Fat BPs

CODE TOOL CHEST
#3

steamed veggies with tofu

6 oz smoked tofu or firm tofu, cubed
3 cups broccoli
2 cups yellow squash
1 cup green beans
4 1/2 tsp slivered almonds, toasted
Spike or herb seasoning (optional)
1/2 lemon

Rinse all veggies well and cut into bite-size pieces. Place veggies and tofu in steamer. Heat small skillet to medium-high. Toss in almonds and stir frequently. Toast until light brown. Immediately transfer almonds to a side dish. Continue steaming vegetables and tofu for a total of 15 minutes or until vegetables are tender. Add Spike or herbed seasoning, if desired. Squeeze the juice of lemon over veggies and tofu and sprinkle with toasted almonds. Serve hot.

3 Protein BPs
3 Carbohydrate BPs
3 Fat BPs

CODE TOOL CHEST

#2

tofu hot dogs with lentils

2 tofu (soy) hot dogs
1/2 cup canned lentils, rinsed and drained
1/2 cup white mushrooms, chopped
6 tb onion, chopped
5 tb celery, chopped
1/4 cup stewed tomatoes
1/4 cup fat-free vegetable broth
salt, pepper, minced garlic, or Tabasco
3 tb avocado, cubed
2 oz soy cheese, grated

Simmer first 7 ingredients together in a saucepan until veggies are tender and lentils and tofu hot dogs are hot. Season to taste with any of the following: salt, pepper, garlic, or Tabasco. Serve garnished with grated soy cheese and avocado.

3 Protein BPs
3 Carbohydrate BPs
3 Fat BPs

CODE TOOL CHEST
#2

smoked salmon, just right

2 100% Wasa rye crackers
2 tb light cream cheese (Neufchâtel)
4 1/2 oz smoked salmon
1 tsp capers
1 red onion, thinly sliced
1/2 cup pineapple, cubed or sliced

Spread cream cheese on crackers. Place salmon, capers, and thinly sliced red onion on top.
Serve pineapple on the side.

3 Protein BPs
3 Carbohydrate BPs
3 Fat BPs

CODE TOOL CHEST
#3

barbeque tofu with pineapple slaw

Barbeque Sauce:
1 tb apple cider vinegar
2 tb tomato paste
1 tb Worcestershire sauce
1 tsp prepared mustard
1/4 tsp stevia powder
1 clove garlic, minced
2 tb water

nonstick cooking spray
6 oz firm tofu, drained and patted dry

Pineapple Slaw Dressing:
2 tb apple cider vinegar

1 tsp white miso
1 tsp tamari
1 tsp sesame oil
1/4 cup water

Pineapple Slaw:
1 1/2 cups green cabbage, shredded
1 1/2 cups red cabbage, shredded
1/4 cup carrot, peeled and grated
1/2 cup red onion, peeled and thinly sliced
1/2 cup pineapple chunks

1 stalk green scallion, sliced

Heat oven to 400 degrees. In small container whisk together ingredients for barbeque sauce. Slice tofu into 1/4-inch rectangles. Spray shallow baking dish with nonstick cooking spray. Lay tofu slices in baking dish. Brush tofu with barbeque sauce on all sides. Place in oven. Cover and bake for 30 to 40 minutes. While tofu is baking, mix together all ingredients for Pineapple Slaw Dressing. Set aside. In small bowl combine red and green cabbage, carrot, onion, and pineapple. Pour dressing over vegetables and stir to blend. Refrigerate until tofu is finished baking. Serve pineapple slaw on plate with hot tofu and garnish with scallion.

Note: Pineapple slaw will last up to one week in the refrigerator and can be made ahead of time. You might want to double or triple the recipe to have extra on hand.

Note: Marinating the tofu for a longer period of time will make it even more flavorful — 3 to 4 hours is ideal.

3 Protein BPs
3 Carbohydrate BPs
3 Fat BPs

CODE TOOL CHEST
#1

tofu with veggies and ricotta

4 oz marinated tofu (in one or two slices)
1 tsp olive oil
1/2 cup onion, chopped
1 cup zucchini, washed and chopped
salt, pepper, garlic, and dried basil, to taste
1 1/4 cups frozen spinach, cooked and well-drained
1/2 cup tomato sauce
1/4 cup skim ricotta cheese

In a nonstick saucepan on medium-high heat, sauté tofu on both sides in 1/3 tsp olive oil until golden. Set aside. In a separate pan, sauté onion and zucchini in remaining 2/3 tsp olive oil, adding salt, pepper, basil, and garlic to taste. When veggies are tender, add cooked spinach. Adjust seasonings. Top tofu with sautéed veggies. Spoon tomato sauce over veggies and sprinkle with ricotta cheese. Cover and heat thoroughly before serving.

3 Protein BPs
3 Carbohydrate BPs
3 Fat BPs

CODE TOOL CHEST

#3

smokey tofu stir-fry

nonstick cooking spray
1 cup green beans
2 cups yellow squash
1 1/2 cups red onion
6 oz firm smoked tofu, cubed
Spike seasoning
1 1/2 tsp tahini

Spray nonstick spray in medium-size skillet. Rinse green beans and cut off tips. Rinse squash and cut into bite-size rounds. Peel and slice red onion into thin slivers. Heat skillet on medium heat. Add red onions and sauté for 1 minute. Add yellow squash, green beans, and smoked tofu. Season with Spike and sauté until vegetables are tender. Serve with tahini drizzled over the stir-fry.

3 Protein BPs
3 Carbohydrate BPs
3 Fat BPs

CODE TOOL CHEST
#2

boca burger chili

nonstick cooking spray
1 1/2 patties Boca Burger Original
1 1/2 cups onion, chopped
1 cup green bell pepper, washed and chopped
2 cups mushrooms, wiped clean and sliced
1/2 cup salsa
1/4 tsp chili powder
1 clove of garlic, finely minced
1/4 tsp Italian seasoning
1 tsp olive oil

Spray skillet with nonstick cooking spray. Heat skillet on medium heat. Add onion, bell pepper, and mushrooms. Sauté for approximately 3 minutes or until onions turn translucent. Crumble Boca Burger into mixture. Add salsa, chili powder, garlic, Italian seasoning, and olive oil. Cook until heated thoroughly. Serve in a bowl.

3 Protein BPs
3 Carbohydrate BPs
3 Fat BPs

CODE TOOL CHEST

#2

lemon grass chicken and veggies

nonstick cooking spray

3 oz of chicken

lemon pepper, to taste

1 carrot, diced

3 cups bok choy leaves, washed

1 tsp ginger, grated

1 1-inch piece lemongrass, smashed with the flat side of a chef's knife

1/2 tsp red pepper flakes

1 scallion, chopped

3 cloves garlic, minced

1 1/2 cups snow peas, ends trimmed

1/2 cup mung bean sprouts

soy sauce, to taste

18 peanuts

Cut chicken into bite-size pieces. Spray nonstick cooking spray in skillet. Season chicken with lemon pepper. Cook chicken on medium-high heat until cooked through. Add carrot, bok choy, ginger, lemongrass, red pepper flakes, scallion, garlic, and 1/4 cup of water. Cook with lid on for 5 minutes. Add snow peas and mung bean sprouts for one more minute of cooking. Season with soy sauce, to taste. Remove the lemongrass and serve. Top with peanuts.

3 Protein BPs
3 Carbohydrate BPs
3 Fat BPs

ZonePerfect
dinners

table of contents:

asian hack chicken salad

Salad:

3 oz boneless cooked chicken,
   shredded into bite-size pieces

1/4 cup celery hearts, thinly sliced

1/2 cup red cabbage, shredded

1/2 cup green cabbage, shredded

1/2 cup grated carrot

1/2 cup cucumber, seeded, peeled, and
   thinly sliced

5 cups red leaf lettuce, washed and
   torn into bite-size pieces

6 roasted peanuts, chopped

1 tb fresh cilantro, finely chopped

1 mandarin orange, peeled and sectioned

1 tsp fresh mint leaves, finely chopped

Dressing:

1/2 tsp natural peanut butter

1 tb lime juice

1 tb mirin (rice cooking wine)

1 tb brown rice vinegar

1/2 tsp sesame oil

1 tb soy sauce

1/2 tsp hot chili paste or
   1/2 jalapeno pepper, seeded and chopped

1 tsp fresh ginger, minced

For the Dressing: Whisk together peanut butter and all liquid ingredients. Add chili paste and fresh ginger.

For the Salad: In a medium bowl, toss chicken with celery, cabbage, carrots and cucumbers. Add dressing a little at a time. Arrange lettuce on plate. Mound chicken and vegetables on top. Sprinkle with peanuts. Garnish with cilantro, orange sections, and mint.

3 Protein BPs
3 Carbohydrate BPs
3 Fat BPs

CODE TOOL CHEST

#1

beef tenderloin with shallot mustard sauce over frisee salad

3 oz beef tenderloin, trimmed of fat
salt and pepper, to taste
olive oil spray
1 shallot, peeled and cut into thick rounds
5 cups frisee or curly endive, washed and
   torn into bite-size pieces
1 tb golden raisins or 1 tb dried cherries
1/2 pear, peeled, cored,
   and cut into 1 1/2-inch x 1/4-inch slices

1/2 cup fennel bulb, washed, trimmed,
   and cut into thin slivers
1 tsp olive oil
1 tb pear vinegar
1 tb balsamic vinaigrette
1/2 cup chicken or beef stock, low-fat variety
1/2 tb Dijon mustard
1 tsp grainy mustard

Heat oven to 425 degrees. Coat beef on all sides with salt and pepper. Place in a skillet with an oven-proof handle over medium-high heat. Spray with olive oil. When very hot, add meat. Sear on all sides until browned. Transfer pan to oven for 10 minutes. Add shallots to pan and return to oven for 15 to 20 minutes more, or until meat thermometer registers 135 degrees for medium-rare. Remove beef from pan.

While tenderloin is baking, arrange frisee, raisins, sliced pear, and fennel on dinner plate. Sprinkle with pear vinegar and olive oil.

Place the pan with the shallots over medium heat. Deglaze shallots by adding balsamic vinegar. Add stock and simmer until shallots are slightly reduced, 2 to 3 minutes. Reduce heat to low. Stir in Dijon and grainy mustard. Keep sauce warm until serving.

Cut beef into 1/2-inch-thick slices. Top salad with beef and drizzle with Shallot-Mustard sauce.

3 Protein BPs
3 Carbohydrate BPs
3 Fat BPs

CODE TOOL CHEST

#1

grilled tuna salad with orange avocado salsa

Salsa:

1/2 naval orange
1/4 cup red onion, chopped
1/2 cup tomato, cut into 1/4-inch pieces
1/4 jalapeno pepper, seeds removed and minced
1 tb cilantro, chopped
1 tb freshly squeezed lime juice
pinch of salt
1/8 tsp freshly ground black pepper
1 tb avocado, sliced

Tuna Salad:

1 cup summer squash, washed, cut into 1/2 moons
1 cup green beans, washed, ends trimmed
dash of lemon thyme
1/4 tsp tarragon
dash of lemon pepper
4 1/2 oz fresh tuna steak
pinch of black pepper
nonstick cooking spray
3 cups mixed salad greens, washed
2/3 tsp olive oil
1 tb raspberry vinegar

Peel orange. Remove seeds and slice into small pieces. Put all remaining salsa ingredients into small bowl and stir to combine.

Spray medium skillet with non-stick cooking spray. Heat skillet on medium-high heat. Add summer squash, green beans, and herbs to skillet. Cook vegetables, stirring occasionally until tender but still brightly colored. While vegetables are cooking, heat a small skillet on medium-high for tuna.

Sprinkle both sides of tuna steak with freshly ground black pepper. Spray pan with light coating of nonstick cooking spray. Grill tuna until done. Cut into thin strips. Assemble plate with mixed field greens topped with grilled vegetables and tuna.

Spoon salsa on top of tuna. Whisk together raspberry vinegar and olive oil and drizzle over salad.

3 Protein BPs
3 Carbohydrate BPs
3 Fat BPs

CODE TOOL CHEST

#1

granny's apple cabbage surprise

nonstick cooking spray
3/4 cup red onion, finely chopped
2 cups red cabbage, shredded
1/4 tsp caraway seeds
1 Granny Smith apple, peeled, cored, and diced
1/8 tsp freshly ground black pepper
1/4 cup vegetable broth
1/8 cup red wine vinegar

In medium saucepan, spray nonstick cooking spray. Cook onions over medium heat for about 5 minutes or until onions are soft. Stir in shredded red cabbage, caraway seeds, diced apples, and freshly ground black pepper. Add vegetable broth and red wine vinegar. Cover saucepan. Cook for 5 to 10 minutes until cabbage is slightly tender but still crisp. Serve warm.

Tip: This dish is great served with grilled chicken, pork tenderloin or venison.

3 Carbohydrate BPs

CODE TOOL CHEST
#2

Kristy says: "It's hard to get all your Carbohydrate BPs for a meal from a salad. This is one reason it's important to learn how to prepare a variety of cooked vegetables and use them for your Carbohydrate BPs."

savory and cool cucumber mint salad

1/2 cup plain yogurt
1/4 cup fresh mint, minced
1 hot chili pepper, minced
1/2 tsp cumin
1 large red leaf lettuce, washed
2 cups cucumber, sliced
1 1/2 cups ripe, fresh peach, peeled, if desired, and sliced
1/4 cup scallion greens, minced

In a small bowl combine yogurt, minced mint, minced hot chili pepper, and cumin to make a salad dressing. Set aside.

Place 1 washed, large lettuce leaf on a dinner plate. Arrange sliced cucumber and sliced peach on top of lettuce. Pour salad dressing on top of peach and cucumber. Sprinkle with minced scallion.

Tip: Serve this recipe with 1/2 cup cottage cheese to complete the 3 Protein BPs.

Tip: This dish would be good as an accompaniment to smoked salmon or seared tuna.

1 Protein BP
3 Carbohydrate BPs

CODE TOOL CHEST
#2

sensible green beans with adventurous artichokes

nonstick cooking spray
1 cup green beans, washed
8 cherry tomatoes, washed
1 1/2 cups artichoke hearts, canned in water, drained
olive oil spray
3 medium cloves garlic, peeled and thinly sliced
1 tsp fresh rosemary, minced
1 tb tamari
2 tb balsamic vinegar
freshly ground black pepper, to taste
salt, to taste
2 tb parmesan cheese

Preheat oven to 425 degrees. Spray baking sheet with nonstick cooking spray. Spread vegetables on the sheet. Spray light mist of olive oil over vegetables. Mix together thinly sliced garlic, minced rosemary, and tamari. Sprinkle over vegetables. Bake about 20 minutes, occasionally turning the vegetables.

Transfer cooked vegetables to serving dish. Drizzle balsamic vinegar over the vegetables. Season with salt and pepper, to taste. Serve warm topped with parmesan cheese.

Tip: You can use 1/8 tsp garlic powder in place of the 3 garlic cloves.

Tip: This dish goes well with fish, fowl, wild game, or venison.

1 Protein BP
3 Carbohydrate BPs
1 Fat BP

CODE TOOL CHEST
#2

bold and beautiful
cajun okra

nonstick cooking spray
3/4 cup red onion, peeled and sliced
1 cup fresh okra, washed and stems trimmed
1 cup sunburst or yellow squash, washed and cut in bite-size pieces
2 tomatoes, quartered
Tabasco sauce, to taste
1 tsp olive oil
Spike seasoning or your favorite seasonings, to taste

Heat skillet to medium-high. Spray with light mist nonstick cooking spray. Add sliced red onion. Sauté for about 1 minute. Add bite-size pieces of sunburst or yellow squash and okra. Sauté for 1 to 2 minutes more. Add tomatoes, a dash of Tabasco sauce, olive oil, and a sprinkle of Spike. Cover skillet and let the vegetables steam for another 3 to 4 minutes. Serve immediately with more Tabasco sauce, if desired.

Tip: This dish goes well with baked tofu or chicken.

3 Carbohydrate BPs
3 Fat BPs

CODE TOOL CHEST
#2

brassy baby summer squash

nonstick cooking spray
1 1/2 cups purple or yellow onion, peeled and sliced
1 cup baby sunburst squash, washed and
    trimmed at both ends or cut into 1/8-inch or 1/16-inch slices, if full grown
1 cup baby patty pan squash, washed and
    trimmed at both ends or cut into 1/8-inch or 1/16-inch slices, if full grown
1 cup frozen green beans or fresh green beans
lemon pepper and salt, to taste
3 to 4 tb water
1/8 tsp dried marjoram
1/8 tsp dried thyme
1 tsp fresh parsley, chopped (optional)

Heat skillet to medium-high. Spray with nonstick cooking spray. Add sliced onion. Sauté until onion becomes soft. Add squash, green beans, and lemon pepper. Add 3 to 4 tb water and marjoram, thyme, and salt to taste. Cover skillet and let vegetables steam for a few minutes until they're tender. Serve with sprinkling of parsley on top, if desired.

Tip: If baby squash is unavailable, regular, grown-up squash will do just fine.

Tip: This dish goes well with chicken, salmon, or soy burgers.

3 Carbohydrate BPs

CODE TOOL CHEST
#2

olive oyl's spinach sauté

1 tb plus 2 tsp raisins
nonstick cooking spray
3/4 cup yellow onions, chopped
4 cloves garlic, minced
1 1/2 cups fresh mushrooms, wiped clean and sliced
10 cups fresh spinach, washed and de-stemmed
1 tb tamari

Soak raisins in enough water to cover them for a few minutes. Spray large skillet with nonstick cooking spray. Sauté chopped yellow onions until onions are soft. Add mushrooms, minced garlic, and raisins. Sauté for another few minutes. Add spinach leaves. Sprinkle vegetables with tamari. Turn heat under skillet to low and cover. Let vegetables cook until spinach is wilted but still bright green. Serve immediately.

Tip: This dish is great with 1 oz feta cheese sprinkled over the top of it. 1 oz feta cheese = 1 Protein BP.

Tip: Greens are readily available year-round, particularly October through April. Choose crisp, fresh leaves with vivid color. Avoid yellowing or wilted vegetables. Store in plastic bags or a vegetable crisper in the refrigerator for 3 to 4 days. Greens can be eaten raw or cooked and are superior sources of Vitamins A and C, iron, riboflavin, calcium, and fiber.

Tip: This dish is delicious with grilled chicken or baked fish.

3 Carbohydrate BPs

CODE TOOL CHEST

#2

brussels sprouts with an attitude

1 1/2 cups Brussels sprouts, washed and ends trimmed
1 tb lemon juice
1 tsp red wine vinegar
lemon rind, finely grated
salt and fresh ground pepper, to taste

In a medium pot, barely cover the Brussels sprouts with water. Bring to a boil, put a lid on the pot, and cook them for about 7 minutes until they're just tender. (They should have a bright green color.) While Brussels sprouts are cooking, mix together lemon juice, vinegar, and finely grated lemon rind. Drain Brussels sprouts. Transfer them to a serving plate. Drizzle lemon juice mixture over Brussels sprouts. Add salt and pepper to taste.

Tip: Add variety to this dish by sprinkling vegetables with caraway seed or cumin while cooking.

Tip: This dish goes well with chicken, beef, turkey, or tofu.

1 Carbohydrate BP

CODE TOOL CHEST

#2

Kristy says: "Write down everything you plan to eat in one meal so you don't forget an important Balanced Portion. Do this for each meal of the day. If you have a meal, which you've especially enjoyed, you can refer back to what you've written in your daily food journal and prepare it again."

scalloped turnips

(Serves 4)

3/4 cup yellow onion, thinly sliced
nonstick cooking spray
4 cups turnips, peeled and thinly sliced
2 tb unbleached oat flour
1 tsp nutmeg
1 cup 1% milk
4 tb light sour cream
1/2 cup nonfat plain yogurt
salt and pepper, to taste

Preheat oven to 350 degrees.

Lightly sauté onions in nonstick skillet until tender. Set aside.

Spray nonstick cooking spray in one-quart casserole dish to lightly coat bottom and sides. Layer 1/3 of turnips in casserole. Top with 1/3 of onion. Sprinkle with 1 tb oat flour, 1/3 tsp nutmeg, and a pinch of salt and pepper. Repeat layering twice.

Mix milk, light sour cream and nonfat yogurt in separate bowl. Pour over turnips. Cover and bake in preheated oven for 30 minutes. Remove cover. Bake for 25 minutes more or until vegetables are tender.

1 cup = 1 serving
Each serving contains:
1/4 Protein BP
1 Carbohydrate BP
1 Fat BP

tempting turnips

1/2 cup onion, chopped
2 cups turnips, peeled and thinly sliced
1/2 tart apple, cored and chopped
2 tsp curry powder
salt, to taste
3 tb light sour cream
nonstick cooking spray

Heat skillet to medium-high. Add nonstick cooking spray to the hot skillet. Sauté chopped onion, stirring frequently until it begins to brown. Stir in peeled and sliced turnips. Cook vegetables about 5 more minutes, adding a little water, if necessary. Add chopped apples, curry powder, and salt. Cover and cook all ingredients until they are tender. Transfer to serving dish. Top with light sour cream.

Tip: This dish is good with roast beef or another type of red meat, such as venison.

3 Carbohydrate BPs
3 Fat BPs

CODE TOOL CHEST
#2

fast and sassy fennel

5 cups salad mix, washed
1 orange, peeled and cut into 1/2-inch slices
3/4 cup fennel bulb, thinly sliced lengthwise
1 tsp olive oil
1 tb tarragon vinegar

In small bowl, combine salad mix, orange slices, and fennel. Whisk together oil and vinegar to make dressing. Toss well and serve.

Tip: Raw fennel has a distinct licorice taste and becomes more delicate when cooked. Look for firm, white, crisp bulbs with white to light green leaf stalks and fresh tops.

Tip: This dish goes well with grilled chicken or shrimp tossed with the salad.

3 Carbohydrate BPs
3 Fat BPs

CODE TOOL CHEST
#2

tangy tomato delight

2 large, ripe tomatoes
1/2 tsp dried oregano or any combination of Italian spices
1/4 tsp garlic powder
salt, to taste
freshly ground black pepper, to taste
2 tb Parmesan cheese
olive oil spray

Preheat broiler. Rinse and dry tomatoes, then cut in half. Place tomatoes on a baking sheet, cut-side up. Sprinkle tomatoes with oregano, garlic powder, salt, pepper, and Parmesan cheese. Spray tomato halves with a very light coating of olive oil. Place tomatoes under broiler and broil them until they are soft but firm and cheese has melted. Watch carefully. Broiling time varies.

Tip: This dish is good when accompanied by beef or chicken entrées.

1 Protein BP
1 Carbohydrate BP

CODE TOOL CHEST

sunny mediterranean holiday vegetables

nonstick cooking spray

olive oil spray

3/4 cup eggplant, washed, cut in half lengthwise, and thinly sliced

1 cup red bell pepper, washed and sliced in thick strips or chunks

1 cup zucchini, washed and sliced lengthwise in thick strips

1 cup yellow squash, washed and sliced lengthwise, 1/4-inch thick

8 cherry tomatoes

1 tsp minced garlic

1 tsp fresh basil, chopped

1 tsp fresh oregano, chopped

2 tb balsamic vinegar

salt and pepper, to taste

Heat large skillet or griddle to medium-hot. Spray with nonstick cooking spray. Lay vegetables on skillet without overlapping. Grill vegetables on one side until they start to turn brown. Then flip the vegetables, spray with light mist of olive oil to equal 1 tsp, and sprinkle with minced garlic, balsamic vinegar, basil, oregano, salt, and pepper. When vegetables are evenly browned on both sides, remove them from the heat. Serve warm.

Tip: When buying eggplant, look for firm, shiny, unwrinkled skin. This means it's fresh.

Tip: You can sprinkle 1 to 3 oz feta or skim mozzarella cheese on top of vegetables as they're in the final stages of grilling. Remember, this adds 1 to 3 Protein BPs to your meal.

Tip: This dish is tasty when it accompanies fish, tofu, shrimp, scallop, or chicken entrées.

3 Carbohydrate BPs
3 Fat BPs

CODE TOOL CHEST

#2

warm and cozy winter vegetables

3/4 cup yellow onion, peeled and quartered
1 1/2 cups turnips, peeled and quartered
1/2 cup carrots, peel and sliced
3/4 cup Brussels sprouts, washed, ends trimmed and halved
olive oil spray
1/2 tsp caraway seeds

Preheat oven to 400 degrees. Place all vegetables into an oven-safe baking dish. Spray with a light mist of olive oil. Toss in caraway seeds. Cover pan and roast vegetables for 45 minutes to 1 hour or until they're tender when pricked with a fork.

Tip: Roasting brings out the natural sweetness of any vegetable. Spraying a little oil on the vegetables helps to lock in their moisture.

Tip: This dish goes nicely with roasted chicken or game hens.

3 Carbohydrate BPs

CODE TOOL CHEST

#2

Kristy says: "Plan ahead for your meals. You'll have all the ingredients on hand and be ready to prepare your naturally healthy ZonePerfect recipes in minutes."

steamed and peppered broccoli florets

1 tsp tahini
1/4 cup vegetable broth
1 tb lemon juice
1 1/2 cups broccoli florets, washed
nonstick cooking spray
1/2 cup each red and orange bell pepper, washed and cut into strips
1 cup yellow bell pepper, washed and cut into strips
1/2 cup yellow squash, washed and cut diagonally in half-moons
1/3 cup canned water chestnuts, drained and rinsed
2 cloves garlic, minced
1/4 cup green scallions, chopped
1 tsp lemon pepper
1 tsp black sesame seeds, toasted

In a small bowl combine tahini, vegetable broth, and lemon juice. Set aside.

Steam broccoli florets in vegetable steamer until they turn an even, bright green. Heat a skillet to medium-hot. Spray skillet with nonstick cooking spray. Add bell pepper strips, squash, water chestnuts and minced garlic. Sauté for 2 minutes. Add steamed broccoli florets and chopped green scallion. Sauté for another 2 minutes.

Place vegetables on a serving plate. Pour tahini, vegetable broth, and lemon juice mixture over vegetables and season with lemon pepper. Sprinkle toasted sesame seeds on top. Serve warm.

Tip: This dish is excellent paired with tofu, chicken, or beef.

3 Carbohydrate BPs
3 Fat BPs

CODE TOOL CHEST

#2

sun and surf hawaiian bok choy

1 1/2 cups bok choy leaves and stalks, washed
nonstick cooking spray
1/2 cup red onion, peeled and sliced into quarter wedges
1 1/4 cups red bell pepper, cored and cut in strips
1 tsp toasted sesame oil
1/8 cup dried hijiki (Japanese seaweed), washed, soaked, and drained
1/2 cup pineapple, cubed
2 tb pickled ginger
Bragg Liquid Aminos or light soy sauce, to taste

Cut bok choy into bite-sized pieces.

Spray nonstick cooking spray on medium-sized skillet. Heat to medium-hot. Toss in quarter wedges of red onion. Sauté for 2 minutes. Add red bell pepper strips, sesame oil, and hijiki. Sauté vegetables for 1 more minute. Add bok choy, pineapple, and pickled ginger to the other vegetables. Sauté 2 more minutes. Remove skillet from the heat. Drizzle with Bragg Liquid Aminos or light soy sauce, to taste. Serve hot.

Tip: This dish is good with broiled tofu or salmon.

2 Carbohydrate BPs
2 Fat BPs

CODE TOOL CHEST
#2

savvy swiss chard with ginger butternut squash

1 tb apple cider vinegar
1/4 tsp red pepper flakes
2 tsp ginger, grated
3 tb orange juice
nonstick cooking spray
6 1/2 cups red Swiss chard, leaves and stems, washed and trimmed
    into 2-inch strips
2/3 cup butternut squash, steamed and sliced
1/4 cup arame (Japanese seaweed available in natural food stores
    or Asian grocers), soaked and drained
3 tsp walnuts

Whisk together vinegar, red pepper flakes, ginger and orange juice. Set aside. Heat large sauté pan on medium. Spray with nonstick cooking spray. Sauté red Swiss chard with steamed butternut squash and arame. Toss with vinaigrette. Top with walnuts. Serve hot or cold as a side dish.

Tip: Swiss chard comes in red, green, and rainbow varieties that are all mild and delicious.

Tip: Kale or spinach can be substituted for Swiss chard in this recipe, but you'll need larger quantities for the spinach and smaller quantities for the kale to equal 1/2 Carbohydrate BP of Swiss chard.

3 Carbohydrate BPs
3 Fat BPs

CODE TOOL CHEST
#2

spaghetti squash with ratatouille

(Serves 4)

1 1/2 cups onion, thinly sliced	3 or 4 cloves garlic, peeled and minced
4 tb olive oil	2 tb red wine vinegar
1 1/2 cups eggplant, washed and cubed	1/2 tsp dried basil
2 cups zucchini, washed and cubed	1/2 tsp dried oregano
1 cup summer squash, washed and diced	salt and pepper, to taste
1 cup green pepper, diced	1 large spaghetti squash
4 large tomatoes, washed and diced	1 cup skim mozzarella, grated
1 cup tomato sauce	8 tb Parmesan cheese, grated

Sauté onions with 4 tb olive oil. Add other vegetables except tomato and tomato sauce. Sauté until just soft. Add tomato, tomato sauce and garlic. Cook about 30 minutes, on low heat, covered. Uncover and add red wine vinegar. Cook down until some of the liquid has evaporated. Season with herbs, salt, and pepper, to taste. As ratatouille is cooking prepare spaghetti squash.

To prepare spaghetti squash, cut into quarters, seed, and place in a large saucepan, rind-side down, with 1 1/2 cups water. Cover tightly. Steam over medium heat for 25 minutes. Remove squash. Scrape pulp with a fork. Divide ratatouille into 4 servings and serve over top of 1 cup of spaghetti squash. Sprinkle each serving with 2 tb of parmesan cheese and 1/4 cup mozzarella cheese.

Tip: This ratatouille is good hot or cold. It makes an excellent filling for omelets.

1 serving ratatouille with one cup spaghetti squash contains:
3 Protein BPs
3 Carbohydrate BPs
3 Fat BPs

CODE TOOL CHEST

#1

turkey over spaghetti squash

nonstick cooking spray
3/4 cup onion, chopped
3/4 cup red pepper, washed and chopped
1 clove garlic, minced
3 oz turkey breast cutlet, cut into strips
1/2 cup stewed tomatoes
dried oregano, basil, and cayenne pepper, to taste
salt and pepper, to taste
1 cup spaghetti squash, steamed
1 tsp olive oil

Spray skillet with nonstick cooking spray. Heat skillet over medium-high. Add onion, pepper, garlic, and turkey. Cook until turkey browns on all sides, stirring constantly. Add tomatoes, herbs, and spices. Reduce heat to low and cook, stirring often until turkey is fully cooked. Adjust seasonings, as desired. Serve over hot spaghetti squash and drizzle with olive oil.

3 Protein BPs
3 Carbohydrate BPs
3 Fat BPs

CODE TOOL CHEST
#1

Kristy says: "Start where you are and do the best you can. You don't have to be perfect to succeed."

steamed collard greens

4 cups collard greens, washed
sea salt, to taste
1 bay leaf
several drops lemon juice or umeboshi vinegar (available at natural foods stores)

Trim 2 to 3 inches from collard stems and wash leaves well. Chop crosswise into thin pieces. Place collard pieces, salt, and bay leaf in small saucepan. Add small amount of water. Steam over low heat until bright green. Drain and remove bay leaf. Sprinkle with lemon juice or umeboshi vinegar.

Tip: 2 cups cooked collard greens = 4 cups raw = 1 Carbohydrate BP

Tip: Steamed collard greens taste good with turkey, chicken, smoked tofu, and soy burgers.

1 Carbohydrate BP

CODE TOOL CHEST

#2

Kristy says: "You're doing great! It's getting easier every day to cook vegetables. Soon it will be effortless. Aren't you enjoying these new tastes? Isn't it a colorful sight to see how green vegetables remain when they're steamed? They're filled with nutrients for your body. Doesn't this make you feel good to know you're taking such good care of yourself and those you love?"

tofu spinach lasagna

1 cup tomato sauce
3 tb cooked chickpeas
1 clove garlic, minced
1 tsp olive oil
salt and pepper, to taste
2 oz marinated firm tofu, thinly sliced
1 1/2 cups frozen spinach, thawed and well-drained
1/2 cup skim ricotta cheese
2 tb parsley, chopped

Simmer tomato sauce, chickpeas, garlic, olive oil, salt, and pepper in a saucepan over low heat for 10 minutes. Set aside.

Preheat oven to 375 degrees. In a small baking dish, place 1 layer of thinly sliced tofu. Top with 1/2 of the thawed spinach and 1/2 of the tomato sauce mixture. Top that with 1/2 the ricotta cheese. Repeat another layer of tofu, followed by remaining spinach, tomato mixture and ricotta cheese. Bake for 20 minutes. Serve garnished with chopped parsley.

3 Protein BPs
3 Carbohydrate BPs
3 Fat BPs

CODE TOOL CHEST
#1

oriental vegetable stir fry

3/4 cup yellow onion
2 cups kale, washed
1 1/2 tsp toasted sesame oil
1 cup mushrooms, wiped clean and sliced
salt and pepper, to taste
1/3 cup water chestnuts
1/4 cup vegetable broth
1 tb Bragg Liquid Aminos or light soy sauce
1 1/2 tb arrowroot
1 1/2 cups snow peas, washed

Cut onion in half lengthwise, peel, then cut in half crosswise and slice thinly. Slice kale into thin strips. Heat sesame oil over medium heat in large skillet or wok. Sauté onions for 3 to 5 minutes. Add sliced mushrooms along with salt and pepper, as desired. Sauté for 2 to 3 minutes. Add kale. Sauté for 2 to 3 minutes more. Add water chestnuts. Toss them together with the other vegetables, cover the skillet or wok, and steam for 2 to 3 minutes.

Combine vegetable broth with Bragg Liquid Aminos or light soy sauce and arrowroot. Stir until arrowroot is dissolved. Pour this mixture over vegetables while stirring. Add snow peas. Simmer for 1 minute or until arrowroot thickens. Serve hot.

Tip: This combination of vegetables, seasonings, and arrowroot creates an authentic Asian appearance, texture, and taste.

Tip: Arrowroot is a thickening agent, like cornstarch, that can be used in equal amounts.

Tip: This dish makes a good accompaniment to tofu, chicken, or turkey.

3 Carbohydrate BPs
3 Fat BPs

CODE TOOL CHEST
#2

orange almond tofu stir-fry

Tofu Marinade:

6 oz firm tofu

1 tsp garlic, freshly chopped

1 tsp ginger, freshly grated

2 tb scallion, chopped

1/2 tsp toasted sesame oil

2 tb soy sauce

1 tsp parsley, freshly chopped

1 1/2 tsp slivered toasted almonds

Stir-Fry Vegetables:

nonstick cooking spray

1 cup button mushrooms, wiped clean and sliced

1 cup raw red pepper, thinly sliced

1 1/2 cups broccoli florets

1/3 cup sliced, canned water chestnuts, drained and rinsed

1/2 tsp toasted sesame oil

1 tsp orange extract

2 tb soy sauce or Tamari

1 tb ginger, grated

3/4 cup snow peas, washed

Drain tofu, pat dry with a towel, and cut into bite-size squares. Combine all other ingredients except parsley. Mix well. Add tofu. Marinate while preparing stir-fry vegetables.

Heat skillet over high heat. Spray skillet with nonstick cooking spray. Add mushroom and red pepper. Stir-fry 1 minute. Add marinated tofu. Stir-fry 2 minutes. Add broccoli and water chestnuts. Sprinkle with oil and other seasonings. Stir often until vegetables appear tender but not overcooked. (This should only take 1 or 2 minutes!) Add snow peas during last minute of cooking.

Serve with slivered toasted almonds. Garnish with chopped parsley.

3 Protein BPs
3 Carbohydrate BPs
3 Fat BPs

CODE TOOL CHEST
#1

tofu stuffed peppers

2 large, round green peppers, washed, tops and seeds removed
nonstick cooking spray
2 cups mushrooms, wiped clean and sliced
3/4 cup onion, peeled and chopped
4 oz marinated baked firm tofu, finely chopped
garlic salt, pepper, chili powder, and cumin, to taste
15 black olives, chopped
1/4 cup tomato sauce
1 oz skim mozzarella cheese, grated

Preheat oven to 350 degrees. Prepare peppers and set aside.

Spray skillet with nonstick cooking spray. Sauté mushrooms and onions over medium-high heat about 5 to 7 minutes, until mushrooms have completely released their liquid. Stir constantly. Remove from heat.

Add tofu, seasonings, black olives and tomato sauce to the mushrooms and onions. Mix well. Stuff tofu mixture into peppers. Place in small baking dish with water to cover up to 1-inch of the bottom. Cover with foil and bake for 35 minutes. Remove foil. Top peppers with grated cheese. Continue to bake for an additional 5 to 10 minutes or until peppers are tender and cheese is melted.

3 Protein BPs
3 Carbohydrate BPs
3 Fat BPs

CODE TOOL CHEST

tofu with black beans, fresh mozzarella, and tomatoes

2 oz firm tofu, cut into cubes
2 oz fresh part-skim mozzarella cheese, cut into cubes
1/2 cup cooked black beans
1 cup ripe cherry tomatoes, washed and halved
1 small clove garlic, finely minced
2 tb fresh basil leaves, minced
1 tb balsamic or Italian vinaigrette dressing
1 tb fresh chives, minced

Mix together tofu, cheese, beans, and tomatoes. Add garlic, basil, and vinaigrette.
Toss to coat. Serve garnished with chives.

3 Protein BPs
3 Carbohydrate BPs
3 Fat BPs

CODE TOOL CHEST
#2

tofu with kidney beans

1 tsp canola oil
1 1/2 cups leeks (white parts only), chopped and rinsed well
1 1/4 cups red pepper, washed and chopped
6 oz marinated extra-firm tofu, cut into bite-size pieces (any style
    marinated tofu, such as Oriental, Italian, or Mexican)
1/4 cup cooked kidney beans
salt and pepper, to taste
1 tb parsley, minced
2 1/4 tsp sunflower seeds, toasted

Add canola oil to skillet and heat on medium-high. Sauté leeks and red pepper for 3 minutes.
Add tofu and kidney beans. Reduce heat to medium-low and cook until beans and tofu are
heated thoroughly. Season to taste with salt and pepper. Garnish with chopped parsley and
toasted sunflower seeds.

3 Protein BPs
3 Carbohydrate BPs
3 Fat BPs

CODE TOOL CHEST

#2

Kristy says: "You're probably going to start noticing weight loss when you
put on your clothes. They'll fit looser, and you'll know you're losing inches."

basic white wine vinaigrette

5 1/2 tb white wine vinegar
1 1/2 tb extra virgin olive oil
1/4 to 1/2 tsp Dijon mustard
1 small clove garlic, finely minced
salt and pepper, to taste

Using a wire whisk, blend vinegar with olive oil and mustard in a small bowl. Add garlic and season with salt and pepper, to taste. Makes 7 tb dressing.

Tip: This dressing is excellent when tossed with your favorite blend of salad greens. Mix up a batch and store in a glass jar in the refrigerator to have on-hand for a quick salad. Just shake to blend and pour.

2 Fat PBs per tablespoon

CODE TOOL CHEST
#3

sesame ginger marinade

5 1/2 tb brown rice vinegar
1 tb expeller-pressed light sesame oil
1/2 tb expeller-pressed toasted sesame oil
1 tsp fresh ginger, finely minced
1 to 2 tsp reduced-sodium soy sauce, or to taste
pinch of white pepper (optional)

Using a wire whisk, blend together the vinegar and both oils. Whisk in the ginger and soy sauce. Add white pepper, if using. Makes 7 tb marinade.

Tip: Delicious as a marinade for beef, chicken, or shrimp. Give it a try!

2 Fat BPs per tablespoon

CODE TOOL CHEST
#2

tempeh and tofu with green beans, mushrooms, and oranges

1 1/2 oz soy tempeh
1/3 cup orange juice
1/2 tsp cornstarch
1/2 tsp reduced-sodium soy sauce
1/4 tsp Worcestershire sauce
1/4 tsp natural, unseasoned rice vinegar
1 1/2 tsp sesame oil, divided

1 cup mushrooms, wiped clean and sliced
1/4 cup green beans, washed and cut
    into 2-inch pieces
garlic powder, to taste
4 oz firm tofu, crumbled
1/4 orange, white pith removed, chopped
salt and pepper, to taste

Steam tempeh over water for 20 minutes. Set aside to cool. Preheat oven to 250 degrees. In a small bowl, mix orange juice with cornstarch. Set it near the stove. In another small bowl, mix together soy sauce, Worcestershire sauce, and vinegar. Brush onto both sides of tempeh. In a large nonstick skillet, heat 1/2 tsp sesame oil. Cook tempeh over medium heat on both sides until lightly browned. Remove to a plate and keep warm in oven.

Meanwhile, add remaining 1 tsp sesame oil to skillet. Sauté mushrooms over medium-high heat. Stir constantly for 5 minutes as mushrooms release their liquid. Add green beans, garlic powder, crumbled tofu, and oranges. Continue to sauté for 5 more minutes, reducing heat as necessary, until green beans are crisp and tender. Give the orange juice mixture a good stir and pour over the vegetables. Stir over medium heat until slightly thickened. Season to taste with salt and pepper. Pour this mixture over warm tempeh and serve.

3 Protein BPs
3 Carbohydrate BPs
3 Fat BPs

CODE TOOL CHEST

#1

tempeh chili with veggies

1 tsp olive oil
1 large clove garlic, minced
3 tb onion, chopped
1/4 cup green pepper, washed and chopped
1/4 cup zucchini, washed and chopped
1/4 cup yellow squash, washed and chopped
1/4 cup tomatoes, chopped
1 1/2 oz soy tempeh, crumbled (Sea Veggie Tempeh, if available)
1/2 cup tomato sauce
1 tsp to 1 tb chili powder, or to taste
salt and pepper, to taste
Tabasco sauce, to taste
2 oz low-fat cheese, grated
1/4 cup mild, medium, or hot salsa

In a nonstick skillet, heat oil. Add garlic and onion. Sauté 2 minutes. Add pepper, zucchini, yellow squash, and tomatoes. Sauté 5 minutes. Add crumbled tempeh and tomato sauce. Season to taste with salt, pepper, chili powder, and Tabasco. Simmer over low heat for 1/2 hour. Stir frequently. Sprinkle with cheese and top with salsa. Serve hot.

3 Protein BPs
3 Carbohydrate BPs
3 Fat BPs

CODE TOOL CHEST
#1

fruity scallops

1 cup cucumbers, washed and sliced
3/4 cup jicama, peeled and sliced
1/2 pear, cored and thinly sliced
1/2 cup grapes, washed
1 oz low-fat mozzarella cheese, cut into small pieces
1 tb walnuts, finely chopped
2 tb good-quality balsamic vinegar, or to taste
3 oz scallops
salt and pepper, to taste

Prepare fruit and cheese salad by mixing cucumbers, jicama, pear, grapes, cheese, and walnuts with balsamic vinegar. Set aside.

Prepare scallops by skewering on a wooden or metal skewer. Season to taste with salt and pepper. Grill or cook scallops on an indoor nonstick grill or pan. Turn them often. When scallops are cooked (only takes a few minutes, depending on the size of the scallops), remove them from the skewer. Put cooked scallops on top of fruit salad.

3 Protein BPs
3 Carbohydrate BPs
3 Fat BPs

CODE TOOL CHEST
#1

baked salmon on fennel with mustard dill sauce

nonstick cooking spray
3 oz salmon fillet
1 tb dry white wine
salt and pepper, to taste
1 tb shallot, peeled and finely chopped
1 cup fennel bulb, thinly sliced
2/3 cup red potato, peeled and sliced
1 oz feta cheese
1 tsp fresh dill, chopped

Mustard Dill Sauce:
1 tb fat-free low sodium chicken broth
1 tb lite mayonnaise
1 tb lemon juice, freshly squeezed
1 tsp spicy brown prepared mustard
salt and pepper, to taste

Preheat oven to 425 degrees. Spray a light mist of cooking spray on the bottom of a small oven-proof dish. Lay salmon, skin side down, in dish and sprinkle with white wine, salt, and pepper. Top with shallots. Set aside.

Spray saucepan with nonstick cooking spray. Heat over medium heat. Add fennel. Sauté for 2 to 3 minutes. Add potatoes. Season with salt and pepper. Add 1/2 cup water to pan. Simmer for 5 minutes. After vegetables have simmered, transfer to baking dish with salmon. Cover with foil. Bake at 425 degrees for 20 minutes or until fish flakes easily when tested with fork.

While fish is baking, prepare Mustard Dill Sauce by stirring all ingredients together until well blended. Pour sauce over fish. Crumble feta cheese on top. Garnish with fresh dill. Serve immediately.

3 Protein BPs
3 Carbohydrate BPs
3 Fat BPs

CODE TOOL CHEST
#1

pineapple mahi mahi

4 1/2 oz filet Mahi Mahi fish
1 tb lemon or lime juice
1 tb soy sauce
garlic, minced, to taste
1/2 cup pineapple chunks
1/4 cup plus 2 tb black beans
2 tb red pepper, minced
1/3 tsp olive oil
6 asparagus spears
2 macadamia nuts, crushed

Marinate fish in lemon or lime juice, soy sauce, and garlic for 20 to 30 minutes. When ready, grill over hot coals or on an indoor nonstick grill, turning once until done.

While fish is grilling, mix pineapple chunks with black beans and minced red pepper. Set aside.

Prepare asparagus by rinsing, then sautéing in a nonstick pan coated with 1/3 tsp olive oil. Cook just until tender and very bright green.

To assemble, put grilled fish on a plate. Top fish with pineapples, black beans, and red peppers. Surround fish with asparagus. Garnish with crushed macadamia nuts.

3 Protein BPs
3 Carbohydrate BPs
3 Fat BPs

CODE TOOL CHEST

pan-sautéed sea bass with capers and olives

4 1/2 oz sea bass filet
   (red snapper or grouper may be substituted)
salt, to taste
freshly ground black pepper, to taste
nonstick cooking spray
3/4 cup red onion, peeled and thinly sliced
1/2 cup yellow squash, washed
   and cut into half-moons
1 cup water-packed artichoke hearts, drained
1 cup zucchini, washed and cut into half-moons
1/4 cup kidney beans, drained and rinsed
1/8 tsp dried marjoram

1/8 tsp dried thyme
lemon pepper, to taste
1 tsp capers
1 tb roasted red bell pepper, chopped
1 tsp lemon juice
1/4 tsp lemon rind, finely grated
1 tsp chive or scallion, finely minced
10 black olives, pitted and quartered
1 tsp parsley, chopped
1 1/2 tsp slivered almonds toasted
lemon wedge for garnish

Season sea bass filet with salt and pepper. Heat a nonstick skillet over medium heat. Spray with nonstick cooking spray. Place filet, skin-side down, in pan. Sauté for 4 minutes. Turn filet over and cook another 3 to 4 minutes.

As filet is cooking, heat another skillet to medium-high heat. Spray with cooking spray. Add sliced red onion to skillet. Sauté until onion becomes soft. Add squash, artichoke hearts, zucchini, kidney beans, marjoram, thyme, and lemon pepper to sautéed onions. Cover skillet. Let vegetables steam a few minutes until they are tender. Remove fish from pan and keep warm.

Toss all remaining ingredients (except chopped parsley, almonds, and lemon wedges) with pan drippings in the fish skillet. Stir to warm. Spoon this mixture over the fish. Garnish with lemon wedges, chopped parsley, and toasted almonds. Serve with sautéed vegetables.

3 Protein BPs
3 Carbohydrate BPs
3 Fat BPs

CODE TOOL CHEST

#1

snappy asparagus grill

12 asparagus spears
nonstick cooking spray
1/2 tsp orange peel, finely grated
juice of 1/2 lemon
lemon pepper, to taste
salt, to taste

Wash and snap ends from asparagus spears. Heat a large cast iron skillet or griddle to medium hot. Spray with a light mist non-stick cooking spray. Add asparagus. Sprinkle with finely grated orange peel. Grill asparagus, turning them occasionally until tender. Add salt and lemon pepper, as desired. Serve warm.

Tip: 1/2 tsp chervil is a nice addition to this dish.

Tip: This dish would go well with trout or salmon.

1 Carbohydrate BP

CODE TOOL CHEST

#2

"Being in the health profession for twenty years has led me to many diets and food programs. The ZonePerfect Nutrition Program plus natural and organic foods has been so successful in balancing my blood sugar and supporting my energy levels. It's truly a lifestyle, and I'm so happy with my results."
Charlotte L., RMT, CCT

pan-seared ruby red trout with lemon and pepper

Trout:
4 1/2 oz ruby red trout fillet
1/2 lemon, cut into quarters
coarsely ground black pepper, to taste
salt, to taste
1 cup Swiss chard, washed and steamed

Skillet Vegetable Medley:
nonstick cooking spray
1 cup leeks, sliced and rinsed well

1 cup yellow squash, washed, cut in half moons
1 1/2 cups artichoke hearts, packed in water, drained
8 cherry tomatoes
1 tsp olive oil
1/2 tsp fresh thyme
4 garlic cloves, minced
1/2 lemon
1 tb capers

Rinse trout fillet and pat dry. Place in shallow dish. Heat nonstick skillet on high heat. Drizzle fillet with juice from 1/4 of lemon, salt, and pepper. Place skin-side-down on hot pan. Cover and cook for 3 minutes until fish flakes easily from its skin. Do not overcook. In the last minute, toss in Swiss chard on top of fish to wilt. Squeeze with juice of remaining 1/4 of lemon. Serve with Skillet Vegetable Medley.

Spray skillet with nonstick cooking spray. Heat on medium-high heat. Add leeks, yellow squash, and artichoke hearts. Sauté for 3 minutes. Add cherry tomatoes, olive oil, garlic, lemon juice, and capers. Sauté approximately 4 minutes more or until cherry tomatoes split open. Serve immediately with Ruby Red Trout.

3 Protein BPs
3 Carbohydrate BPs
3 Fat BPs

shrimp sauté with chickpeas

1 tsp olive oil
6 tb onion, chopped
2 cloves garlic, minced
1/2 cup mushrooms, wiped clean and chopped
1/2 cup green pepper, washed and chopped
1/2 cup cherry tomatoes, washed and halved
1/2 cup broccoli florets, washed
1/4 cup cooked chickpeas
1/3 cup water chestnuts, drained and rinsed
4 1/2 oz jumbo shrimp, peeled, de-veined
salt, pepper, and curry powder (optional), to taste
2 tb cilantro or parsley, chopped

In large nonstick skillet, sauté onion, garlic, mushrooms, green peppers, and tomato halves for 5 minutes. Stir frequently. Add broccoli. Continue to cook for 5 more minutes, stirring. Add chickpeas, water chestnuts, and shrimp along with salt, pepper, and curry powder, if using. Cook until shrimp are completely done. Serve garnished with chopped cilantro.

3 Protein BPs
3 Carbohydrate BPs
3 Fat BPs

CODE TOOL CHEST

#1

tandoori chicken with cucumber yogurt sauce

2 1/2 oz boneless chicken breast
3 tsp toasted pine nuts

Marinade:
1 clove garlic, minced
1 tsp lemon juice
1/2 tsp ginger, grated
1/4 tsp ground cumin
1/4 tsp paprika
1 pinch cayenne pepper
1/4 tsp cardamom, ground

Cucumber Yogurt Sauce:
2 cups cucumber,
    peeled and chopped into 1/4-inch chunks
1 orange, peeled and sliced into 1/4-inch slices
1 tb red onion, chopped
1 tb fresh dill, chopped
4 tb plain low-fat yogurt
1 tb red wine vinegar

Blend together all marinade ingredients. Pat mixture onto chicken. For best results, let chicken marinate in refrigerator for at least 4 hours.

Heat skillet or grill to medium-high heat. Grill or pan-sear chicken for 8 minutes per side or until no longer pink at center and juices run clear. Serve with Cucumber Yogurt Sauce and top with toasted pine nuts.

For the Cucumber Yogurt Sauce: Combine all ingredients in small bowl. Mix until blended. Serve chilled with cooked chicken.

3 Protein BPs
3 Carbohydrate BPs
3 Fat BPs

CODE TOOL CHEST
#1

zesty lemon-paprika chicken with snow pea and radish salad

3 oz boneless, skinless, chicken breast
lemon juice from 1/2 lemon
salt and pepper, to taste
1/8 tsp paprika
1/2 tsp lemon peel, grated
nonstick cooking spray
1/2 tsp parsley, finely chopped for garnish
2 lemon rounds for garnish, thinly sliced

Place chicken breast in a glass baking dish. Squeeze juice of 1/2 lemon over chicken. Sprinkle with salt, pepper, paprika, and lemon peel. Heat nonstick skillet to medium-high. Spray skillet with light mist of cooking spray. Sauté breast one side at a time until browned on both sides, approximately 5 minutes per side. Lay lemon rounds on chicken. Sprinkle with parsley during last few minutes of cooking.

Slice and serve chicken hot or cold on top of Snow Pea and Radish Salad with Minted Ginger Vinaigrette.

>

Snow Pea and Radish Salad:

1 1/2 cups snow peas, washed, ends removed

1/3 cup canned, sliced water chestnuts,
    drained and rinsed

1/2 cup carrot, peeled and grated

2 radishes, washed, ends trimmed and thinly sliced

3 cups bib lettuce, washed, dried, and torn
    into bite-size pieces

1 tsp fresh mint, minced

Minted-Ginger Vinaigrette:

1 tsp almond oil

1 tb rice vinegar

1 tsp mirin or cooking sherry

1 tb orange juice, freshly squeezed

1 tsp orange peel, finely grated

1 tsp hot prepared mustard

1 tsp ginger, freshly grated

salt, to taste

freshly ground black pepper, to taste

Steam snow peas about 2 minutes until just crisp, tender, and bright green. Immediately plunge snow peas into ice bath to keep them from cooking further. Drain snow peas in colander. Pat dry with towel and set aside.

In small bowl whisk together vinaigrette ingredients. Set aside.

Arrange bib lettuce on serving plate. Mound snow-peas, water chestnuts, carrots, and radishes onto the lettuce. Drizzle with vinaigrette and sprinkle with mint.

3 Protein BPs
3 Carbohydrate BPs
3 Fat BPs

CODE TOOL CHEST

grilled lime chicken
with roasted rosemary vegetables

Marinade:
3 tb lime juice, freshly squeezed
1 clove garlic, chopped
1/4 tsp dried red pepper flakes

3 oz boneless chicken breast

Roasted Rosemary Vegetables:
2 cups broccoli florets
nonstick cooking spray
3/4 cup onion, sliced
3/4 cup fennel bulb

6 medium-size asparagus spears
1 cup zucchini, sliced
1/2 cup radicchio, sliced
1 tsp olive oil spray
1/4 tsp rosemary
1/8 tsp sage
1/4 tsp marjoram
1/4 tsp lemon thyme
2 garlic cloves, peeled and minced
1/2 tsp sea salt
2 tb lemon juice

Marinade: Mix lime juice with garlic and pepper flakes. Place chicken breast in a glass pan and pour marinade over chicken. Refrigerate marinating chicken while preparing roasted and grilled rosemary vegetables.

Roasted Vegetables: Rinse all vegetables well. In small saucepan bring 2 cups of water to a boil. Add broccoli florets and blanch for two minutes or until broccoli turns bright green. Drain under cold running water to prevent further cooking. Set aside. Spray large skillet with nonstick cooking spray. Set heat to medium high. Place all vegetables evenly on surface of pan. Spray vegetables with light spritz of olive oil to equal one teaspoon. Blend all herbs, garlic, and lemon juice together. Stir into vegetables. Cook until slightly charred.

Chicken: While vegetables are cooking, heat small skillet on high. Spray skillet with nonstick cooking spray. Add chicken and marinade. Cook until browned on both sides. If chicken is still pink on the inside, reduce heat and cook until juices run clear. Serve chicken with roasted vegetables.

3 Protein BPs
3 Carbohydrate BPs
3 Fat BPs

CODE TOOL CHEST
#1

pan-seared pork tenderloin atop arugula and apple salad with curry dressing

2 cups mixed field greens, washed

1 cup arugula, washed, trimmed, and torn into bite-size pieces

1/4 cup celery, chopped

1/2 tart apple, cored and sliced (drizzle with lemon juice to keep from discoloring)

1/2 tb raisins

1 oz feta cheese, crumbled

nonstick cooking spray

2 oz pork tenderloin, visible fat removed

salt and coarsely ground black pepper, to taste

1/2 cup red onion, finely sliced

1/2 cup red grapes, washed

1 tb balsamic vinegar

Curried Dressing (2 servings):

2 tsp olive oil

2 tb red wine vinegar

1 clove garlic, finely minced

1/8 tsp dry mustard

1/8 tsp ground cumin

1/8 tsp curry powder

freshly ground black pepper, to taste

Arrange arugula, field greens, chopped celery, raisins, and crumbled feta cheese on salad plate. Heat skillet to high. Spray skillet with nonstick cooking spray. Sprinkle tenderloin on each side with coarse ground pepper and salt. Sear pork on each side for approximately 2 minutes. Turn heat down to medium-high. Continue cooking for 3 more minutes on each side. Add sliced onion and grapes. Sauté until onion is soft and grapes begin to split. Add balsamic vinegar. Sauté 30 more seconds. Pork is done when thickest part is a medium to light pink color. Remove pork from pan. Slice on the diagonal into 1/4 inch slices.

Whisk all dressing ingredients together in a bowl. Top salad with onion and grape mixture and pork slices. Drizzle with 1/2 of the curried dressing. Serve immediately.

3 Protein BPs
3 Carbohydrate BPs
3 Fat BPs

CODE TOOL CHEST

#1

pork tenderloin with apples, beets, and green beans

3 oz lean pork tenderloin
1 clove garlic, sliced
salt and pepper, to taste
1 tsp olive oil
1 tsp fresh rosemary, minced, or 1/4 tsp dried rosemary
1/2 apple, sliced
1/2 cup steamed beets, sliced
1 cup green beans, washed and steamed
balsamic vinegar, to taste

With a sharp paring knife, make sliver holes in the pork and stuff slices of garlic into them. Rub the pork with salt, pepper, olive oil, and rosemary. Sauté in a nonstick pan using olive oil spray, if necessary.

While pork is cooking, arrange apples, beets, and green beans on a plate. Drizzle with balsamic vinegar, if desired. Slice pork and serve along side of salad.

3 Protein BPs
3 Carbohydrate BPs
3 Fat BPs

CODE TOOL CHEST
#1

Kristy says: "Use a food scale at home to weigh items. When you eat at a restaurant, it will be easier to remember how a 3 or 4-Balanced Portion is supposed to look."

beef burger on rye with citrus salad

4 1/2 oz lean ground beef (10 to 15% fat)
salt, pepper, onion powder, garlic powder, to taste
1/2 tsp Worcestershire sauce
nonstick cooking spray
1 slice 100% rye bread
1/2 tb light mayonnaise
1 piece green leaf lettuce, washed and dried
1 slice tomato
1 to 2 tsp lemon or lime juice
fructose, a pinch
1/4 grapefruit, sliced with pith removed
1/4 orange, sliced with pith removed
3/4 tsp slivered almonds

Mix ground beef with spices and Worcestershire sauce. Form into a patty. Spray a nonstick pan with olive oil spray. Cook patty in pan until done, turning once.

While patty is cooking, spread lite mayonnaise on the rye bread. Top with lettuce and tomato slice. Set aside.

Prepare the citrus salad: In a small bowl, mix together the lemon or lime juice with a pinch of fructose. Add the fruit and toss gently. Serve the burger with fruit that is garnished with almonds.

3 Protein BPs
3 Carbohydrate BPs
3 Fat BPs

CODE TOOL CHEST
#2

beef stew for two

(Serves 2)

6 oz lean beef stew meat, cubed

4 tsp cornstarch

2 tsp olive oil

3/4 cup onions, chopped

1/3 cup red potatoes, scrubbed, rinsed, and cubed

1 cup carrots, peeled and chopped

salt and pepper, to taste

1 cup tomatoes, washed and chopped

1 bay leaf

1 clove garlic

1/4 cup red wine

1/2 to 3/4 cup all-natural, fat-free beef stock

In a mixing bowl, toss cornstarch with cubed beef. In a nonstick pot, heat olive oil. Sear meat for 2 or 3 minutes, stirring often. Add onions, potatoes, and carrots. Season to taste with salt and pepper. Sauté for 3 minutes. Add tomatoes, bay leaf, garlic, wine, and 1/2 cup stock. Bring to a boil. Cover and reduce to low. Simmer until meat is very tender, adding more stock if necessary. Adjust seasonings before serving.

Each serving contains:
3 Protein BPs
3 Carbohydrate BPs
3 Fat BPs

CODE TOOL CHEST

#1

lamb with greens and winter squash

3 oz lamb meat, cut into bite-size pieces
1 tb red wine
1/2 tsp olive oil
1 tsp fresh mint leaves, minced
salt and pepper, to taste
6 tb onion, chopped
1/2 tsp olive oil
3 cups collard greens, washed and cut into bite-size pieces
2 to 4 tb fat-free chicken or vegetable stock
2/3 cup steamed butternut squash

Marinate lamb in the wine, olive oil, mint, salt, and pepper for at least 30 minutes, if possible. In a nonstick skillet, sauté lamb until cooked.

While lamb cooks, sauté onion in 1/2 tsp olive oil in nonstick skillet for 5 minutes. Add greens and stock. Cook, partially covered, over low heat for 10 or more minutes, until leaves are bright green but tender to chew. Season to taste.

Serve lamb over hot, steamed butternut squash surrounded by mounds of bright green collard greens.

3 Protein BPs
3 Carbohydrate BPs
3 Fat BPs

CODE TOOL CHEST
#1

venison and black bean chili for two

(Serves 2)

6 oz ground venison meat (or diced venison meat)
1 tsp olive oil
1/2 cup cooked black beans
1 cup stewed tomatoes
1 cup water
3/4 cup onions, chopped
1 cup green pepper, chopped
2 cloves garlic, minced
1/2 jalapeno pepper, seeded and minced (optional)
1 tb chili powder, or to taste
salt, pepper, cumin, and oregano, to taste
1/2 cup salsa
3 tb light sour cream

Brown venison meat in olive oil in a nonstick skillet over medium-high heat. Add remaining ingredients, except salsa and sour cream, stirring well. Reduce heat to low, cover and cook for about 45 minutes, stirring occasionally. Add water, if necessary. Serve garnished with salsa and light sour cream.

Each serving contains:
3 Protein BPs
3 Carbohydrate BPs
3 Fat BPs

CODE TOOL CHEST
#1

ZonePerfect
snacks

table of contents:

goat cheese and rye crackers

1 oz goat cheese
3 Finn Crisp rye crackers or 2 light rye crackers
5 black olives, pitted and chopped

Spread goat cheese on crackers. Top with olives.

1 Protein BP
1 Carbohydrate BP
1 Fat BP

CODE TOOL CHEST

#3

deli turkey with crackers

2 light rye crackers
1/2 tsp tahini
1 1/2 oz deli turkey

Spread tahini on rye crackers. Top with 1/2 of the turkey on each cracker.

1 Protein BP
1 Carbohydrate BP
1 Fat BP

CODE TOOL CHEST
#3

egg salad on rye crackers

1 hardboiled egg
1 tsp light mayonnaise
1 tsp red onion, finely minced
2 tsp celery, finely minced
3 Finn Crisp rye crackers or 2 light rye crackers

Chop egg. Add mayonnaise, onion, and celery. Spoon onto crackers and enjoy!

1 Protein BP
1 Carbohydrate BP
1 Fat BP

CODE TOOL CHEST
#2

mustard, onion, and cheese on rye

1 oz mozzarella or low-fat Swiss cheese, grated
1 tsp red onion, finely minced
2 tsp red pepper, finely minced
1/4 tsp Dijon mustard
1/2 piece 100% rye bread
1 tb guacamole (page 173)

Mix cheese with minced onion and pepper. Set aside.

Spread mustard over bread. Top with cheese mixture. Melt under a broiler until cheese is bubbly.
Top with guacamole.

1 Protein BP
1 Carbohydrate BP
1 Fat BP

CODE TOOL CHEST
#2

chicken salad for snacks

(Serves 6)

6 oz cooked white chicken meat, cubed or shredded

1 cup celery, chopped

2/3 cup green onions, chopped

2 large dill pickles, chopped

2 tb light mayonnaise

1/8 tsp garlic powder

1/2 tsp celery seed

salt, to taste

1/2 apple or 2 light rye crackers

Mix all ingredients together. Refrigerate. Serve with 1/2 apple or 2 light rye crackers.

Divide chicken salad into 6 equal portions to get 1 BP Protein and 1 BP Fat.

Each serving contains:

1 Protein BP

1 Carbohydrate BP

1 Fat BP

CODE TOOL CHEST

#2

smoked salmon with avocado

1 tb ripe avocado, mashed
1 Wasa rye cracker or two light rye crackers
1 1/2 oz smoked salmon
1 tsp capers, drained

Spread avocado on rye cracker. Top with salmon. Sprinkle capers over salmon.

1 Protein BP
1 Carbohydrate BP
1 Fat BP

CODE TOOL CHEST

#3

the pear and the chicken

1/2 pear
1 oz cooked chicken
1 tsp raspberry vinaigrette
handful mixed lettuce, washed

Arrange lettuce on salad plate. Slice pear and chicken and lay both over bed of lettuce.
Drizzle with raspberry vinaigrette.

1 Protein BP
1 Carbohydrate BP
1 Fat BP

CODE TOOL CHEST

#3

smoked salmon with dill on rye

2 tsp light cream cheese
1 Wasa rye cracker
1 1/2 oz smoked salmon
1 tsp green onion, minced
1/8 tsp fresh dill, minced

Spread cream cheese over cracker. Top with salmon, onion, and dill.

1 Protein BP
1 Carbohydrate BP
1 Fat BP

CODE TOOL CHEST

#3

tomato stuffed with chickpeas and kalamata olives

1 oz low-fat cheddar cheese, cut into small pieces
2 tb cooked chickpeas
3 Kalamata olives, pitted and minced
1 to 2 tsp lemon juice
garlic, minced, to taste
dried oregano and marjoram, a pinch
salt and pepper, to taste
1 whole fresh tomato, scored in quarters but not cut all the way through
balsamic vinegar

Mix cheese with chickpeas, olives, lemon juice, garlic, and herbs. Season to taste with salt and pepper. Stuff mixture into center of tomato. Drizzle with balsamic vinegar.

1 Protein BP
1 Carbohydrate BP
1 Fat BP

CODE TOOL CHEST
#2

tofu pup with avocado

1 tofu hot dog
1 corn tortilla, heated
1 tb ripe avocado, mashed
1 lime wedge

Heat tofu hot dog and corn tortilla in skillet or toaster oven. Spread avocado over tortilla. Squeeze lime juice over avocado. Roll tortilla around tofu hot dog.

1 Protein BP
1 Carbohydrate BP
1 Fat BP

CODE TOOL CHEST
#3

smoked tofu with apple

1/2 apple
1/3 tsp almond butter
2 oz smoked tofu

Spread almond butter on apple. Slice smoked tofu into snack-size pieces.

1 Protein BP
1 Carbohydrate BP
1 Fat BP

CODE TOOL CHEST
#3

tuna and grapes

1 oz water packed canned tuna, drained
pinch celery seed
1 tsp light mayonnaise
1 tb chopped celery
1 tb pickled ginger, diced
1 scallion chopped
1 large romaine lettuce leaf, washed
1/2 cup grapes, washed

Mix tuna, celery seed, mayonnaise, chopped celery, ginger and scallion together. Spoon onto center of lettuce leaf. Wrap lettuce leaf around tuna mixture. Serve with grapes on the side.

1 Protein BP
1 Carbohydrate BP
1 Fat BP

CODE TOOL CHEST
#2

jicama with swiss dip

1/8 cup hummus
1 tb guacamole*
1 oz low-fat Swiss cheese, grated
1/2 cup jicama, peeled and cut into finger sticks

Mix hummus with guacamole and cheese. Use as a dip for cold, crispy jicama.

*Guacamole:
1 tb ripe avocado
1/2 tsp lime juice
1 tsp prepared salsa

To make guacamole, mash avocado with lime juice and prepared salsa.

1 Protein BP
1 Carbohydrate BP
1 Fat BP

CODE TOOL CHEST

#2

apple and cheese

1 oz Amish Cheese (yogurt and skim milk cheese)
1/2 apple
3 cashews

Enjoy cheese and apples together, with cashews on the side.

1 Protein BP
1 Carbohydrate BP
1 Fat BP

CODE TOOL CHEST

#3

blueberry cottage cheese

1/4 cup low-fat cottage cheese
1/2 cup frozen or fresh blueberries
3 pistachios

If using fresh blueberries, rinse well. Place cottage cheese in individual serving dish.
Top with fruit and nuts.

1 Protein BP
1 Carbohydrate BP
1 Fat BP

CODE TOOL CHEST

#3

cottage cheese and pineapple

1/4 cup low-fat cottage cheese
1/2 cup fresh pineapple chunks
1 macadamia nut, chopped

Add pineapple to cottage cheese. Sprinkle with chopped nut.

1 Protein BP
1 Carbohydrate BP
1 Fat BP

CODE TOOL CHEST

#3

spiced pear with ricotta

1/4 cup low-fat ricotta cheese
1/2 ripe red pear, sliced
cinnamon and cardamom, to taste
3 hazelnuts, lightly toasted and crushed

Spoon ricotta cheese onto a serving plate. Top with pear slices.
Sprinkle with cinnamon and cardamom, to taste.

Garnish with hazelnuts.

1 Protein BP
1 Carbohydrate BP
1 Fat BP

CODE TOOL CHEST
#3

cheese and plum

1 plum, washed
1/4 cup ricotta cheese
1 macadamia nut, chopped
cinnamon, to taste

Wash and dice plum.

Mix plum into ricotta cheese with chopped nut.

Sprinkle with cinnamon.

1 Protein BP
1 Carbohydrate BP
1 Fat BP

CODE TOOL CHEST

#3

cucumbers, tomatoes, and cottage cheese

3/4 cup cherry tomatoes, washed and cut in half

1 cup cucumbers, peeled and sliced

1 tb fat-free vinaigrette dressing

1/4 cup low-fat cottage cheese

1/2 tsp chives

1 tsp walnuts, chopped

Toss tomatoes and cucumbers with vinaigrette dressing. Mix cottage cheese with chives.
Spoon over vegetables. Top with walnuts.

1 Protein BP
1 Carbohydrate BP
1 Fat BP

CODE TOOL CHEST

#3

peach crisp with cottage cheese

(Serves 6)

4 ripe peaches, pitted and chopped
2 tsp granulated fructose, divided
cinnamon, to taste
salt, a pinch
1/2 oz rolled oats (dry oatmeal)
1 tsp canola oil
4 1/2 tsp slivered almonds
1 1/2 cups low-fat cottage cheese

Preheat oven to 375 degrees. Mix peaches with 1 tsp fructose, cinnamon, to taste, and just a pinch of salt. Place peaches in a small baking dish. In a small bowl, mix the oats with remaining tsp of fructose. Add canola oil, slivered almonds, a few grains of salt, and more cinnamon, if desired. Mix well. Sprinkle this on top of the peaches. Bake for about 1/2 hour or until peaches are bubbly and mixture is hot. Serve with cottage cheese on the side.

Each serving will be accompanied by 1/4 cup cottage cheese.

Each serving contains:
1 Protein BP
1 Carbohydrate BP
1 Fat BP

CODE TOOL CHEST
#1

cold blueberry macadamia delight

1/2 cup 1% low-fat milk
1/4 cup frozen blueberries
1/2 scoop ZonePerfect Protein Powder (3 1/2 grams)
1 macadamia nut, crushed

Blend milk with berries in a blender. Add protein powder. If desired, add a bit of cold water.
Serve topped with macadamia nut.

1 Protein BP
1 Carbohydrate BP
1 Fat BP

CODE TOOL CHEST

#3

yogurt and almonds

1/2 cup plain low-fat yogurt
1 1/2 tsp slivered almonds

Place yogurt in a cup and sprinkle with almonds.

If desired, add vanilla, orange, maple or strawberry extract.

1 Protein BP
1 Carbohydrate BP
1 Fat BP

CODE TOOL CHEST

#3

tofu pumpkin pie

(Serves 10)

Crust:
8 Wasa Light rye crackers, crushed
cinnamon, a dash
3 tb plus 1 tsp melted butter
1 apple, grated
1/4 tsp stevia powder
    (available at most natural food stores)
1 egg beaten

Filling:
14 oz extra-firm tofu
2 eggs
2 tsp vanilla
2 cups pumpkin, unsweetened
1/4 tsp stevia powder
1/2 tsp sea salt
1 tb pumpkin pie spice

Crust: Preheat oven to 350 degrees. Mix crushed Wasa crackers with cinnamon, butter, grated apple, stevia, and egg. Spray nonstick 9-inch pie pan with light coating of cooking spray. Evenly spread crust mixture into pan with fingers to form crust. Bake 20 minutes. Cool.

Filling: Preheat oven to 350 degrees. Purée tofu, eggs, vanilla, pumpkin, stevia, salt, and pumpkin pie spice in blender or food processor until smooth. Taste. Add more spice, if desired. Pour filling into prepared crust. Bake 35 to 40 minutes. Chill. Filling will firm as it chills.

Each serving contains:
1 Protein BP
1 Carbohydrate BP
1 Fat BP

CODE TOOL CHEST
#1

strawberry sorbet

1 cup frozen strawberries
1 scoop ZonePerfect Protein Powder (7 grams)
2 to 3 ice cubes
1 1/2 tsp slivered almonds

Blend strawberries, protein powder, and ice cubes in a blender. Put in individual serving dish.
Top with slivered almonds.

1 Protein BP
1 Carbohydrate BP
1 Fat BP

CODE TOOL CHEST

#3

soft vanilla custard
with cherries and almonds

(Serves 6)

3 eggs
3 cups 1% milk
2 tsp granulated fructose
1/4 tsp vanilla extract
1 1/2 cups frozen sweet, pitted cherries (no sugar added), thawed
3 tb slivered almonds, lightly toasted

In a large pot, beat eggs well. Add milk, fructose, and vanilla. Heat, stirring constantly over medium-low. Mixture should come to a simmer but not boiling with light bubbles gathering around the edges. Pour into an 8" x 8" square baking dish. Refrigerate until cooled. Top with cherries and slivered almonds.

Each serving contains:
1 Protein BP
1 Carbohydrate BP
1 Fat BP

CODE TOOL CHEST
#2

ZonePerfect bars

1/2 of any of the following bars from ZonePerfect:

Chocolate Raspberry

Double Chocolate

Apple Cinnamon

Chocolate Mint

Lemon Yogurt

Strawberry Yogurt

Chocolate Caramel Cluster

Caramel Apple

Peach Yogurt

Chocolate Vanilla Crème

Fudge Graham

Chocolate Peanut Butter

1 Protein BP
1 Carbohydrate BP
1 Fat BP

CODE TOOL CHEST

#3

ZonePerfect
index